"This book is necessary, informative, relevant, practical, and touching. For those interested in the modern rabbinate and its challenges, this book is heartily recommended. For those already in the pulpit, this book is required reading!"

— **Rabbi Dr. Tzvi Hersh Weinreb**, Executive Vice President, Emeritus, Orthodox Union

"*The Art of Jewish Pastoral Counseling* builds bridges – between pastoral counseling and psychotherapy, between rabbis and their congregants, between religious practice and supportive care. Its teachings are wise and clear in a way that both conveys and yet belies the depth of the thinking underlying them. This book brims with emotional and spiritual intelligence. Read it and leap to a new understanding of counseling in the religious context."

— **David Spiegel, MD**, Willson Professor and Associate Chair of Psychiatry and Behavioral Sciences, Stanford University School of Medicine

"Congregants in crisis routinely turn to faith leaders for guidance. Friedman and Yehuda's book will be of immense assistance to rabbis, pastors and other faith leaders in meeting the needs of those crying in the wilderness of this life."

— **Victor Vieth**, Senior Director and Founder, Gundersen National Child Protection Training Center, Board member, GRACE (Godly Response to Abuse in the Christian Environment)

"Rabbis are constantly confronted with suffering and complex human relationships. Friedman and Yehuda present an excellent foundation for good pastoral work: listening and establishing the necessary conditions that create trust, safety and resilience, being aware of one's own reactions and being able to establish boundaries and limits in order to be of maximal comfort. This is a wonderful addition to the literature."

— **Bessel van der Kolk, MD**, Medical Director Trauma Center at JRI (Justice Resource Institute), Professor of Psychiatry, Boston University School of Medicine

The Art of Jewish Pastoral Counseling

The Art of Jewish Pastoral Counseling provides a clear, practical guide to working with congregants in a range of settings and illustrates the skills and core principles needed for effective pastoral counseling. The material is drawn from Jewish life and rabbinic pastoral counseling, but the fundamental principles in these pages apply to all faith traditions and to a wide variety of counseling relationships.

Drawing on relational psychodynamic ideas but writing in a very accessible style, Friedman and Yehuda cover when, how and why counseling may be sought, how to set up sessions, conduct the work in those sessions, and deal with difficult situations, maintain confidentiality, conduct groupwork, and approach traumatic and emotive subjects. They guide the reader through the foundational principles and topics of pastoral counseling and illustrate the journey with accessible and lively vignettes. By using real-life examples accompanied by guided questions, the authors help readers to learn practical techniques as well as gain greater self-awareness of their own strengths and vulnerabilities.

With a host of examples from pastoral and clinical experience, this book will be invaluable to anyone offering counseling to both the Jewish community and those of other faiths. *The Art of Jewish Pastoral Counseling* will appeal to therapists, particularly those working with Jewish clients, counselors, psychotherapists, psychoanalysts, and rabbis offering pastoral counseling, as well as clergy of other faiths such as ministers, priests, imams, and lay chaplains.

Michelle Friedman, MD, is a psychiatrist and psychoanalyst long involved in bridging religious life and mental health issues. In 1998 Friedman began the pastoral counseling program at Yeshivat Chovevei Torah Rabbinical School. She is now director of that program and associate professor of clinical psychiatry at Icahn School of Medicine at Mount Sinai in New York City.

Rachel Yehuda, Ph.D., is a psychologist and neuroscientist who has conducted research on post-traumatic stress disorder and resilience for over 25 years. Dr. Yehuda has lectured in the Pastoral Counseling program at Yeshivat Chovevei Torah Rabbinical School, where she also served on the board of Directors. She is currently Professor of Psychiatry and Neuroscience at the Icahn School of Medicine at Mount Sinai. She is also the Director of Mental Health at the James J. Peters Bronx Veterans Affairs Hospital.

Psyche and Soul: Psychoanalysis, Spirituality, and Religion in Dialogue Book Series

Jill Salberg, Melanie Suchet & Marie Hoffman
Series Editors

The *Psyche and Soul: Psychoanalysis, Spirituality, and Religion in Dialogue* series explores the intersection of psychoanalysis, spirituality, and religion. By promoting dialogue, this series provides a platform for the vast and expanding interconnections, mutual influences, and points of divergence amongst these disciplines. Extending beyond western religions of Judaism, Christianity, and Islam, the series includes Eastern religions, contemplative studies, mysticism, and philosophy. By bridging gaps, opening the vistas, and responding to increasing societal yearnings for more spirituality in psychoanalysis, *Psyche and Soul* aims to cross these disciplines, fostering a more fluid interpenetration of ideas.

Titles in this series:

Vol. 1: *The Art of Jewish Pastoral Counseling: A Guide for All Faiths* by Michelle Friedman and Rachel Yehuda

The Art of Jewish Pastoral Counseling

A Guide for All Faiths

Michelle Friedman and Rachel Yehuda

Routledge
Taylor & Francis Group

LONDON AND NEW YORK

First published 2017
by Routledge
2 Park Square, Milton Park, Abingdon, Oxon OX14 4RN

and by Routledge
711 Third Avenue, New York, NY 10017

Routledge is an imprint of the Taylor & Francis Group, an informa business

© 2017 Michelle Friedman and Rachel Yehuda

The right of Michelle Friedman and Rachel Yehuda to be identified as author of
this work has been asserted by them in accordance with sections 77 and 78 of the
Copyright, Designs and Patents Act 1988.

British Library Cataloguing in Publication Data
A catalogue record for this book is available from the British Library

Library of Congress Cataloguing in Publication Data
Names: Friedman, Michelle S., author.
Title: The art of Jewish pastoral counseling : a guide for all faiths /
Michelle Friedman and Rachel Yehuda.
Description: New York City : Routledge, 2016. |
Series: Psyche and Soul: Psychoanalysis, Spirituality and Religion in Dialogue ; 1 |
Includes bibliographical references and index.
Identifiers: LCCN 2016021527 | ISBN 9781138690226 (hardback: alk. paper) |
ISBN 9781138690233 (pbk. : alk. paper) | ISBN 9781315535333 (e-book : alk. paper)
Subjects: LCSH: Pastoral counseling (Judaism)
Classification: LCC BM652.5 .F75 2016 | DDC 296.6/1–dc23
LC record available at https://lccn.loc.gov/2016021527

ISBN: 978-1-138-69022-6 (hbk)
ISBN: 978-1-138-69023-3 (pbk)
ISBN: 978-1-315-53533-3 (ebk)

Typeset in Times
by Out of House Publishing

If a man has worry in his heart, let him speak of it to another.

Sanhedrin 100b

Dedicated to Rabbi Dr. Zvi A. Yehuda z"l who taught us that the rabbinic heart is as essential as the rabbinic mind.

Contents

Case vignettes, figures, and table

Examples

Figures

Table

Acknowledgments

Many people contributed valuable suggestions and wisdom to the writing of this book. We thank Dr. Esther Altmann, Dr. Jacob Appel, Emily Belfer, Rachel Belfer, Sarah Belfer, Dr. Kathy Berkman, Sandee Brawarsky, Dr. Alison Estabrook, Rabbi David Fried, Dr. Willard Gaylin, Phil Getz, Dr. Jack Gorman, Tobi Kahn, Rabbi Dov Linzer, Betsy Melamed, Father Kelly-Ray Merritt, Rabbi Yona Reiss, Maya Rosen, Dr. Jill Salberg, Miriam Schacter, Dr. Joseph Triebwasser, Elisheva Urbas, and Barbara Zucker. The *New Yorker* cartoon featured as Figure 6.1 in Chapter 6 is reprinted by permission of Condé Nast.

We appreciate the support of our husbands, Benjamin Belfer and Mitchell Rothschild. Most of all, we thank the faculty, students, and graduates of Yeshivat Chovevei Torah Rabbinical School as well as graduates of other seminaries for their trust in allowing us to shape their pastoral education.

Preface

"This is hard to talk about, but ..."
"Our son is dating someone of another faith."
"I'm gay and I can't keep it a secret from my family any longer."
"My mother is in a coma on life support and I have to make an important decision."
"I'm having a crisis of faith."

Clergy educators and community leaders face these types of personal revelations from congregants, students, acquaintances, and total strangers and are often largely unprepared for the counseling component of their job. Education for religious leadership traditionally focuses on mastery of sacred texts and presumes that study enables future spiritual leaders to help people navigating life events that include unexpected turmoil or catastrophe. Increasingly, it has become clear that the emotional complexity of this work requires an additional and specific skill set. Appropriate pastoral responses are not always intuitive or obvious. They require deliberate education and training. In this book, we draw from our experience educating rabbis and mental health professionals to offer clear, practical, and supportive guidance for spiritual leaders of all faith traditions in their pastoral roles.

Pastoral counseling is care that is given by a spiritual leader and informed by religious and psychological wisdom. For people who are religiously affiliated, this spiritual leader may be the first address for advice or guidance in such moments. Many people turn to clergy because they perceive that their situation requires a religious response. For regular congregants, routine questions regarding religious practice may indicate an underlying need for pastoral counsel.

Those who do not have an established religious affiliation look to clergy for advice around emotionally charged life-cycle occasions.

Most clergy, religious educators, and spiritual community leaders are not formally trained to deal with the pastoral component of their work. Educational standards in pastoral counseling programs are not consistent, and religious seminaries may have minimal, if any, pastoral requirements as a condition of receiving ordination (Goldschein 2015). Although some clergy are innately talented listeners and advisors, those who are not naturally inclined or trained to attend to pastoral needs are likely to stumble through sensitive situations. This may be detrimental to those they are trying to assist. Pastoral counseling training involves learning methods that sometimes require the counselor to suppress natural instincts, such as offering superficial reassurance rather than facilitating expression of feelings. Training also allows leaders to understand how much of their own personal history is appropriate to share when relating to a congregant's situation.

This volume teaches core principles for catalyzing psychological and emotional awareness that leads to competent, effective pastoral behavior. Grounded in both the Jewish tradition and the world of mental health, we explore basic principles of care for others, as well as principles of practitioner self-reflection. The goal for the readers is to develop greater confidence in the ability to navigate tricky pastoral situations. We begin by exploring the basic landscape of pastoral counseling and then look at how it differs from secular mental health treatment. Among other topics are skills for listening, transference/countertransference, borders and boundaries, individual and group dynamics, and confidentiality. We ground theory in practice by illustrating these lessons with case examples that mirror situations that practitioners may face. In doing so, the reader can examine personal strengths and weaknesses. We hope that this self-reflection will increase competence and satisfaction. We then outline key components of a successful intervention, while also alerting readers to potential problems that can result from interactions with congregants. We also address methods of self-care that help prevent clergy burnout. The discussion questions at the end of each case are designed to give you the tools to extrapolate from the examples in the book to real-life situations that you will face.

While the concepts outlined in this book are generalizable to all faith traditions and vocations, the focus is on Jewish clergy, religious educators, and other spiritual community leaders. The examples are drawn from experience and offered largely via four fictional clergy characters.

Chapter 1 presents the obvious first question: "Why turn to a rabbi?" Chapter 2 focuses on the tools that clergy need to help congregants. These include an awareness of the rabbi's internal state, as well as a learned skill set. Chapter 3 details categories of personal conduct that are relevant for pastoral counselors. Chapter 4 examines the structure and meaning of the pastoral interview itself. Chapter 5 suggests how to interpret impressions and data gleaned in pastoral encounters. Chapter 6 expands this perspective into the realm of unconventional but frequent challenges faced by pastoral counselors. Chapter 7 is devoted to a specific challenge – that of confidentiality. The difference between pastoral counseling for individuals and groups is explained in Chapter 8. Chapter 9 contains several multi-layered vignettes.

To date, the majority of Jewish spiritual leaders have been men, reflecting a long historical tradition. Because of a changing reality, we have written this book for men and women across the denominational spectrum. Although much of the material in this book is derived from our experiences educating Orthodox male rabbis, it is applicable to men and women who serve in a broad range of educational, leadership, and pastoral roles. We intend that our readership spans the range of religious perspectives. For those who seek Jewish legal clarification on specific points in the text, we provide endnotes.

For simplicity, the term "rabbi" is used throughout this book. Readers may wish to substitute teacher, principal, camp director, administrator, or chaplain. In fact, the same applies to a priest, minister, imam, or anyone else who assumes a religious leadership position in the context of an interpersonal relationship. Similarly, the expression "interview" is used to define any pastoral encounter whether it is in person, over the phone, or by email. The term "congregant" refers to any person whom a rabbi encounters in an interview.

Reference

Goldschein, Hillel (2015). "Evaluation of an Orthodox Jewish Pastoral Counseling Program," Master's Thesis, Organizational Psychology, Baruch College.

Chapter 1

Turning to clergy for help

Why talk to the rabbi?

Congregants turn to clergy for many reasons. For some, the rabbi represents a moral compass in a time of confusion. The rabbi may be a familiar community leader or a trusted parent figure. For others, the rabbi represents the accrued wisdom of Jewish tradition, a person able to discuss problems from a vantage point of shared values and spiritual outlook. Even when the concern is not a matter of Jewish law, the rabbi may be a source of comfort based on prior relationship. Consider a middle-aged woman facing a marital crisis. A rabbi may have guided her through her bat mitzvah, marriage, and the death of her parents. The woman may now belong to a synagogue with a rabbi who counsels free of charge and welcomes congregants with personal issues in a manner that makes her feel good about seeking religious advice. Turning to her rabbi during a time of distress feels like a natural extension of an established, caring relationship.

Even people who do not have a current religious affiliation frequently consult clergy in anticipation of landmark events such as birth, marriage, and death. Reaching out to clergy may occur during celebratory occasions or when tragedy strikes. For example:

- A young man and woman from different religious backgrounds contact their college rabbi to discuss their upcoming wedding.
- A couple seek out a rabbi when they are expecting their first child in order to plan how they might celebrate this joyous event in some traditional manner, such as a circumcision or baby naming.
- A single parent consults a Jewish educational director on how to plan a bar or bat mitzvah for a child.

- A terminally ill man estranged from Judaism connects with the hospital chaplain and is comforted in knowing that arrangements will be made for him to receive a traditional burial.

People also connect to clergy for instruction on how to navigate their everyday lives without the explicit expectation of pastoral counseling. Their needs can often be met through explanation of religious practice or other time-limited interventions. In addition to influencing congregants' feelings toward Jewish life, rabbinic sensitivity in these moments also contributes to congregants' overall wellbeing.

Sometimes clergy initiate contact.

- Sensing that a worshipper looks unusually preoccupied at morning prayers, the rabbi says, "You look caught up in thought today – would you like to talk for a moment?"
- An adult education teacher makes a mental note to check in with a married couple that bickered unpleasantly during a class.
- A Hillel rabbi sends a friendly email to a college student who has not shown up to services for a while.

Proficiency in pastoral counseling involves being attuned to nuances like those in the above examples. When life's circumstances cause stress or difficulty, pastoral counseling offers a religious context in which spiritual healing can take place. Pastoral counseling sets up a unique sanctuary based on listening, an activity that has become rare in contemporary culture. People regularly reach for their smartphones during dinners, and their attention flickers between email, text messages, and Facebook. In a world where few people sit still and pay full attention to the experience of others, a listening and supportive presence can make a great difference.

The art of listening

In mental health training, much time is devoted to developing the skill of active, compassionate, non-judgmental listening. How well a clinician listens effects all components of the relationship with the patient – the thoroughness of history obtained, the accuracy of hypotheses generated, and the effectiveness of therapeutic interventions offered. Active listening comes about when the mental health professional brings full attention to the session. As the patient speaks, the thera-pist not only listens to the words spoken, but also notes the person's mood, expressions, and body language. This enables the therapist to actively generate ideas that will help the patient process material in a different way.

Compassion is communicated through caring presence. The mental health provider's first task is to create a therapeutic alliance. Such an alliance is formed on a foundation of mutual respect. The therapist refrains from critique or judgment of the patient's beliefs or practices. The therapist is committed to listening to whatever comes up and to working with that material in order to help the patient lead a less con-flicted, happier life. Training programs are designed to hone therapists' listening skills by teaching them to reflect on their sessions with patients. Parsing clinical moments teaches mental health professionals to pay attention to what patients say, as well as to how they say it. This method also highlights key interactions between therapists and patients.

In traditional clergy education, there is a stronger focus on talking and giving advice than on listening. Rabbis are trained to perform ritu-als, deliver sermons, and lead classes. Rabbis are not accustomed to stop talking and listen. It is difficult to convince rabbis that "just" listening actually helps people who have heartbreaking life stories or are facing unfixable situations. Clergy often feel compelled to do or say something in these circumstances. Moreover, clergy may become increasingly anx-ious if they do not make an active intervention. However, sitting quietly and paying full attention to a suffering person *is* doing something pow-erful (Nouwen 1979). Because there is a natural tendency to avoid hear-ing painful experiences, active listening is a skill that must be taught. In the absence of training, listening to a painful experience may generate anxiety sufficient to interfere with appropriate pastoral intervention. Anxiety may cause the rabbi to act prematurely or ineffectively, thus unintentionally sabotaging the interview. Three common barriers pre-vent the rabbi from listening and acting effectively:

- Not being able to listen to negative material because it hits too close to home.
- Being distracted by the intellectual aspects of an inquiry regarding Jewish law or custom and missing latent emotional material.

- Worrying that a congregant's situation may result in a violation of Jewish law or unethical behavior.

Three examples are presented to illustrate how pastoral efforts can succeed or fail depending on how well clergy understand active listening. Throughout this book, questions are provided at the end of each example to help you practice your pastoral counseling skills and think about how the questions influenced your reactions before you read our discussion.

Example 1. An unexpected reaction in the context of a routine hospital visit

Rabbi Daniel Marcus pays a hospital visit to Dana Feldman, a congregant in his synagogue, who is recovering from mild burns sustained a few days earlier. She and her two young children escaped from a fire caused by a gas explosion in their home. At the time of the accident, Dana's husband, Avery, was away on a business trip. After initial greetings, Dana begins to describe how terrified and alone she felt while trying to get her toddler son and small daughter out through the smoke. She starts to cry and says, "Avery should have been here with me. I'll never forgive him for going on that trip."

Rabbi Marcus begins to feel anxious. He expected a routine hospital visit to a congregant who is recovering well but is still a little shaken up. His intent was to reach out to her as a gesture of caring and support. In an attempt to comfort Dana, Rabbi Marcus decides to point out how well she did and how lucky she was. He states, "Dana, you must feel so relieved that everything turned out all right. Your courage is amazing. You saved your children."

Soon afterwards, their conversation dwindles to an uncomfortable halt, and the rabbi leaves.

Rabbi Marcus wonders, "Why did Dana shut down?"

Questions to consider

1. What went wrong in this interview?

2. Did Rabbi Marcus do something that contributed to Dana's shutting down?
3. What were your own feelings as you read this story?

Discussion

Dana shut down because Rabbi Marcus deflected her emotional response when he gave her the compliment about her bravery. Why did he do this? The rabbi praised Dana because he was not prepared that her emotional response to the fire would be anger towards her husband. Rabbi Marcus has a pleasant relationship with Avery and does not think of him in a negative way. While his intention in making the visit was to be kind, Rabbi Marcus ignored Dana's statement about Avery not being there and what that meant for her. This made Dana feel alone. Just as Avery had not been there for her, Rabbi Marcus was not there for her, either. The message sent by Rabbi Marcus, albeit inadvertently, was that he did not want to hear her negative emotions or deal with her anger. Dana shut down because she did not feel heard.

The rabbi's optimal response would be a supportive comment that prompted Dana to share more. He might have said, "That must have been really hard for you," or "Please, tell me more." Even if he was not prepared to deal with Dana's anger towards her husband, he could have recognized her strong feeling. Sitting and listening would have offered pastoral hospitality. While the rabbi's job is not to probe the marriage at this time, his calm presence would validate her distress. By lauding Dana's bravery, Rabbi Marcus implicitly critiqued her anger and closed the door on her talking more openly. His pastoral visit would have been more effective if he had sat quietly and given Dana the opportunity to tell her story.

An untrained rabbi is likely to behave in a similar manner. Rabbi Marcus expected a short visit. The facts known to him before the visit suggested that the situation was fortunate, as no one was severely injured. On some level, Rabbi Marcus felt that Dana was overreacting. After all, can she expect Avery to be home all the time? Rabbi Marcus is not home for his wife and children all the time. Does that mean his wife is angry as well? It all felt like too much for him to think about at the bedside. A compliment about Dana's bravery seemed like the right thing.

When clergy sit with distressed congregants, they may feel that their task is to come up with words or actions that will relieve immediate suffering. Too frequently, a rabbi interrupts a congregant's acute outpouring of emotion with premature advice, reassurance, and nuggets of religious inspiration. While such responses are motivated by a desire to soothe and say something positive, they often reflect anxiety aroused in the rabbi by the congregant's narrative. Anxiety creates a sense of helplessness, and this helplessness promotes a rush to action that leads away from negative emotions. While it might seem counterintuitive that the ability to express painful emotions is an important step towards feeling better, this is the lesson. The rabbi does not serve best by providing compliments or moving people away from negative feelings. The rabbi helps by allowing the congregant to release difficult feelings without interruption, no matter how painful and distressing to the listener. Had Rabbi Marcus listened quietly, he would have communicated to Dana that her anger and fear could be safely expressed and managed. Permission to vent feelings opens the way to finding strategies that lead to recovery.

Pastoral training is designed to help identify barriers to listening. In the above example there were two barriers. First, Rabbi Marcus was caught by surprise at Dana's anger and felt unprepared to respond. Second, he found himself identifying with Avery, whom the rabbi knows and likes. His own feelings prompted him, however inadvertently, to shut down Dana's complaints. Rabbi Marcus should have dealt with these feelings by identifying his reactions to Dana before rushing to make them go away. His premature intervention was a result of his own discomfort. Awareness of these feelings would allow Rabbi Marcus to be fully present for his congregant and provide an optimal pastoral response.

Pastoral issues that involve questions of religious practice

In the above example, Rabbi Marcus's visit with Dana did not involve specifically religious material. However, congregants sometimes present pastoral challenges that involve questions of religious practice. When this occurs, rabbis must broaden their attention to include the Jewish dimension as well as the emotional content. Some rabbis may focus on a point of Jewish law or custom to the exclusion of the emotional content. For some, this arises from a perceived commitment to the primacy of Jewish tradition. They can miss the emotional forest for the religious trees if they narrow their sights in lieu of considering the larger context in which a question was asked.

Example 2. A *halakhic* (legal) question in the context of a traumatic life event

A 24-year-old Jewish soldier, Stuart Lasky, was serving in the U.S. Army in Afghanistan, where his jeep hit a mine. He suffered injuries necessitating an above-the-elbow amputation of his left arm. Several weeks post-surgery, while recuperating in a VA hospital, Stuart asks to see a Jewish chaplain. Rabbi Jack Stein, the Hillel rabbi at the local university, volunteers at the hospital and comes to see the young soldier. After some initial conversation, Stuart poses a question, "Rabbi, it's been a while since I prayed in the morning. I want to put on *tefillin* [phylacteries] again. I asked my parents to bring mine from home. I think that I'm supposed to wrap the *tefillin* around my left arm. How do I go about that now?"

Questions to consider

1. How would you respond to the soldier's question?
2. What other feelings might there be beneath his question?
3. What do you do when you do not know the answer to a religious question?

Discussion

Certainly the rabbi should answer a question requiring clarification of Jewish law if he knows the answer. If Rabbi Stein does not know how Jewish tradition advises in the matter of putting on *tefillin* when the left arm is gone, he should find out as soon as possible and get back to Stuart with the answer. Clergy should never feel embarrassed when they need to consult a text or more senior clergy to adjudicate a question of religious law. Often, they worry that congregants will be annoyed or put off if answers are not readily available. The opposite is more likely to be true. By acknowledging that he does not know the answer and will look it up or ask, Rabbi Stein communicates that he takes the matter seriously enough to spend extra time thinking about Stuart's concern and doing research to get the right information. Stuart will interpret such effort as caring and respectful.

Whether the chaplain knows the answer on the spot or needs to inquire further, he must listen and respond in a way that explores the meaning of the soldier's query. Rabbi Stein allows himself to wonder, "What does this request mean? Why does this young man want to resume putting on *tefillin* now, and what is the relationship to the absent arm? Why and when did he start and stop putting them on? Is there a subtext to his question that I should explore? Is he asking me to inquire how his injury occurred? Is there a moral or psychological injury as well as a physical one? Might Stuart be worrying how women will react to his body and what kind of effect it will have on his romantic life?"

This internal dialogue allows Rabbi Stein to formulate his response, "I'm sorry, I don't know the details of putting on *tefillin* in the case of an amputated arm. But I know whom to ask and will get that answer to you within a day or two. But I also want to tell you how moved I am that after all that you've been through, you want to put on *tefillin*. I want you to know that I am available to talk more if you want to."[1]

Too often, clergy answer the specific question they have been asked and close the conversation. Sometimes, questions of Jewish law are presented to clergy in the unconscious hope that a broader discussion will ensue and that the rabbi will dig into the reason for the inquiry. In the above story, Rabbi Stein must keep in mind that Stuart has likely been through horrific experiences. He may be using the *tefillin* as a cover for other issues that he is scared to bring up. As he listens to the young soldier, Rabbi Stein is likely to feel a mixture of emotions that includes sadness for his injury, curiosity about his religious background, and eagerness to guide him towards greater Jewish affiliation. The degree to which Rabbi Stein is open to his internal thought process will directly affect the flow of his conversation with Stuart. If the rabbi focuses exclusively on answering the "What do I do?" question, he runs the risk of prematurely shutting down a larger conversation in which Stuart might explore his feelings about his injury, his Jewish heritage, and his overall future. Some congregants may think that the rabbi will not be receptive to such issues, while others may not be open to seeing the rabbi as a pastoral counselor. Both kinds of congregants may respond by keeping the conversation limited to the matter of Jewish law. By learning to listen, the rabbi picks up the appropriate cue. The rabbi inquires and lets the congregant lead the way. Similarly, the attuned rabbi decides when to move between listening and giving advice.

In Examples 1 and 2, the pastoral and religious issues do not conflict in any obvious way. An area of particular challenge for some clergy is when a situation involves potential violations of Jewish law. By definition, the rabbi is dedicated to a life of Jewish values and practice. As a representative of that commitment, the rabbi will sometimes be in the position of trying to persuade people to live more religiously committed lives while validating realities that conflict with Jewish tradition. These realities include notions of how to achieve maximal individual happiness amidst shifting social norms. In contrast to mental health providers who are trained to be value-neutral, clergy subscribe to core belief systems. Therefore, a rabbi may worry that a non-judgmental stance will be interpreted as condoning behavior that violates Jewish law. The rabbi may fear that a congregant will perceive empathic listening as implicit permission to continue on a religiously incorrect or even dangerous path. This is not the case. A congregant not looking for a religiously informed answer has many opportunities to seek other forms of counsel. Thus, the rabbi, chaplain, Hillel director, principal, JCC (Jewish Community Center) director, or other Jewish spiritual leader does not compromise his or her principles by listening to life events or choices that are not consistent with traditional practice. In fact, active and compassionate listening is more likely to strengthen their authority and their power as exemplars of religious life. This is especially true when clergy need to navigate potential conflicts between congregants' personal preferences and Jewish tradition.

Example 3. A request for permission to bend the rules

Tova Rosen, a 38-year-old married woman, mother of children ages 14, 11, and 9, and a part-time accountant, makes an appointment with Rabbi Marcus. She and her family belong to a different Orthodox synagogue, but their children attend the same school as

the Marcus children. Tova reveals that she is unexpectedly pregnant, within the first trimester, and is considering an abortion.
However, she feels hesitant from a religious point of view because
she assumes that traditional authorities would not support such
a decision.

Rabbi Marcus listens as Tova tells him that while her health is
good and the family is stable and thriving, another baby was not
in the picture. She was looking forward to resuming work full-
time and pursuing other interests. Finances are also tight. Her
husband says that the decision about whether to continue the
pregnancy is up to her.

Rabbi Marcus is aware of many thoughts and feelings as he
listens to Tova. From a religious/legal point of view, he knows
that opinions differ as to permissibility of terminating pregnancy at forty days or earlier after conception, with some opinions allowing even later.[2] He also detects a note of outrage in
himself; he and his wife have struggled with infertility. Over the
years they have counseled many other infertile couples. He feels
affronted that a woman blessed with a healthy pregnancy would
consider termination.

Questions to consider

1. Why do congregants ask questions of rabbis when they most likely
    anticipate the answer?
2. How do you handle situations when you are not sure what the con-
    gregant wants to hear?

Discussion

Rabbi Marcus takes a moment to consider his reaction to Tova. "Why
is she coming to me? Tova Rosen is well informed religiously. She must
know that an Orthodox rabbi is not likely to support pregnancy termination in this case. She is not even my congregant. What does she
really want from me?" During this critical time of reflection, he has an
insight. "Tova came to talk to me because although I am not her rabbi,
I am an Orthodox rabbi. She could have gone to a therapist who would
likely be more neutral about terminating a healthy pregnancy. Maybe

she wants me to tell her that she must go through with it, to chastise her for even thinking about an abortion."

Rabbi Marcus's awareness of his own reaction to Tova – criticism – helps him modulate his feelings and formulate a response that acknowledges Tova's conflict while also pointing out the paradox of her choice to consult him. Validating Tova's struggle is important, as it establishes a plane of alliance between them. The rabbi's genuine concern, coupled with his religious authority, provides the basis for Tova to trust him and listen to his advice. Rabbi Marcus responds, "I understand that going back to diapers was not what you had in mind and that the costs of raising another child are very real ... I'm also thinking that out of the many people you might have chosen to talk to about your dilemma, you came to see me, an Orthodox rabbi whom you know from our kids' school, not your regular rabbi. I wonder if you expect, even want, me to tell you that Jewish law weighs against you having an abortion. Could it be that in part you hope I will persuade you to have this baby?" Rabbi Marcus and Tova Rosen continue to talk for another half-hour. As the interview comes to a close, Tova says, "Rabbi, thank you for listening. You helped me clarify what's going on."

Rabbi Marcus may have other thoughts regarding Tova Rosen's situation that he does not share with her. For example, he notes her description of the pregnancy as "unexpected." He wonders, was this conception the result of a contraceptive failure? Might Mrs. Rosen feel ambivalent about having another child? More speculative hypotheses include wondering whether the pregnancy resulted from a situation of coerced sex in which birth control was unavailable from the outset. While Rabbi Marcus is aware that a psychotherapist might investigate further, he chooses not to do so, as he feels that such inquiry is inappropriate in his relationship with Tova Rosen and would feel intrusive given the nature of the question she asked.

The more aware clergy are of their own barriers to listening, the freer their minds will be to generate helpful questions. In the context of a pastoral interview, a rabbi has two sets of questions, the ones the rabbi asks out loud and the ones the rabbi keeps to him- or herself. The rabbi's inner dialogue helps formulate questions that inform the interview. The questions the rabbi asks out loud are designed to gather more information. They include straightforward who, what, where, and when questions as well as more general probing comments, such as "Please tell more about ..." or "I want to be sure I understand this better." The kinds of questions running through the rabbi's mind about a congregant include:

1.   Why is this issue coming up now? Has something happened to tip the balance of the congregant's status quo?
2.   Has the congregant experienced anything like this before?
3.   How has the congregant gotten through similar difficulties in the past?
4.   What natural resilience, spiritual resources, or personal supports have been helpful to the congregant before?

At the same time, the rabbi considers questions about his/her role in the situation:

1.   What is my relationship to this person?
2.   How am I reacting to this question and the information I am learning?
3.   What is my role in this interaction?
4.   How can I be of help?

Tools of listening: transference and countertransference

Another tool shared by practitioners of pastoral counseling and mental health professionals is a commitment to try and understand content that lies beneath the surface of what is spoken. Some of that content has already been illustrated in the above examples. Active, compassionate, non-judgmental listening requires paying attention to unspoken material that is embedded within a narrative. Mental health education values and prepares clinicians to read between the lines. This section describes the principles of transference and countertransference as major tools to help access important information about the congregant and the rabbi that may not be conveyed verbally. Simply put, transference and countertransference are reactions of the patient/congregant and therapist/rabbi, respectively, to the therapeutic or pastoral interaction. Transference refers to the activation of a congregant's past emotions, memories, and associations, including physical sensations, onto present-day encounters. Often, some aspect of the current situation, such as the authority of clergy, or a feature of the actual person of the therapist/rabbi, such as their gender, age, voice, or mannerisms, rekindles dormant feelings and memories in the patient/congregant. This dynamic is constantly operative and underscores all human interaction, healthy as well as pathological. Countertransference describes the therapist's/rabbi's counterpart responses to patient/congregant. Patients and congregants trigger cascades of associations for mental health professionals and clergy. Transference and countertransference phenomena are constantly generated during clinical and pastoral encounters. These reactions may arise independently or in concert with one another.

In Example 1, the story of the woman who escaped the fire, Dana shut down after Rabbi Marcus's misplaced compliment about her bravery. The strength of her reaction, i.e. her defensive transference to the rabbi's comment, suggests that earlier feelings of abandonment might have been revived by his comments. In reality, Rabbi Marcus's motive for the visit was genuine caring – exactly the opposite of what Dana felt. However, Dana's transference, based on past experience that had nothing to do with Rabbi Marcus, catalyzed a perceptual distortion on her part. Dana wanted the rabbi to acknowledge her terror at having to deal with her circumstance and validate her anger towards her husband. Instead of feeling proud, she was estranged by his complimenting of her heroism and she withdrew. From his side, Rabbi Marcus's countertransference, in which Dana and her situation kindled experiences and reminiscences of his own, led to his misplaced compliments. Greater attunement would allow him to better understand Dana's heightened reaction, i.e. her transference. If he could recognize, rather than avoid, his own ambivalence about how present husbands are expected to be, Rabbi Marcus would have a wider repertoire of responses. These would include calling Dana up and revisiting their earlier failed interaction.

The ability to identify the nature of transference and countertransference reactions allows clergy and therapists to access highly relevant information in a relatively short period of time. This material helps explore life challenges and pave the way to constructive interventions. Mental health programs dedicate a great deal of time to helping trainees identify and interpret transference and countertransference. So too, clergy benefit dramatically in their pastoral roles from learning these same principles. In addition to an intellectual appreciation of these phenomena, mental health programs require that trainees present detailed accounts of treatment sessions to senior supervisors. Through this process, new therapists learn how to recognize and use the powerful feelings evoked in therapy. Explicit discussion of transference and countertransference phenomena sensitizes therapists to subtle shifts of their emotional pulse that in turn allow a greater range of responses.

Rabbi Marcus thought that Dana was overreacting. On one level, transference of Dana's feelings of abandonment partially explains her intense reaction. At the same time, the compliment that derailed the counseling stems from Rabbi Marcus's reaction to her overreaction, in other words, his countertransference. What we now know about Rabbi Marcus is that he personally identifies with husbands who are not always at home when their wives need them. He felt connected with Avery, but upon seeing the consequences for Dana of Avery's "neglect" and how upset she was, he sought to deflect the emotional intensity in the room rather than staying with it. Thus, Dana's transference response (her overreaction) kindled a reaction in Rabbi Marcus that, when left unacknowledged by him, led him to quell his own anxiety rather than provide a pastoral response. Had he been trained to understand each pastoral response as a potential countertransference, Rabbi Marcus might have recognized that Dana's negative emotions were hitting too close to home for him. This in turn would allow him to give Dana space to vent her anger, which is what she needed from him at that moment.

Rather than reacting to a situation on the surface, the trained rabbi is aware that the multiple levels of feeling generated between him or her and the congregant are a rich source of information about the congregant's personality style and history and are an opportunity to use his or her own feelings as an important tool with which to bring solace. Transference reactions are highly individualized and can be activated by objective characteristics of a rabbi such as age, gender, or appearance. Older rabbis are assumed to be wise. Yet rabbis early on in their careers frequently express surprise that congregants well along in years also turn to them for wisdom and advice. Gender carries a special valence for Jewish clergy. Male rabbis typically conjure traditional paternal associations such as authority and judgment.

Women's spiritual leadership evokes a wide range of feelings in the more maternal realm. Congregants might expect female rabbis to be more receptive, less critical, and better at mediating conflict. From the countertransference perspective, female clergy often note that while their male colleagues are accorded power automatically, women need to actively assert their authority and take power.

The dynamics described above with respect to transference also apply to countertransference. In Example 3, the unexpected pregnancy, Rabbi Marcus identifies his countertransference response – outrage. Paying attention to this response allows him to hypothesize more broadly about Tova Rosen's choice to consult with him. He understands that her visit incorporates an unspoken wish for a religious solution to her dilemma. This example also highlights some of the challenges in examining transference and countertransference phenomena in a rabbinic context. In traditional mental health treatment, the therapist provides the maximum opportunity for the patient to reveal the issues by deliberately creating a climate of neutrality. The therapist does not engage in casual conversation or reveal information that will skew the session in the direction of a personal relationship. Transference is most clearly detectable when the recipient of transferred feeling, i.e. the therapist, is not well known to the patient because the relationship has been deliberately kept focused exclusively on the patient. This degree of anonymity allows transference to flourish, as the patient's reactions are not constricted by real information known about the therapist. In contrast to the therapist, the rabbi is well known to the congregant via multiple communities and social roles. Nonetheless, transference manifestations to the rabbi, while less obvious, will still be present and active.

Congregants respond to the rabbi not only as an authority figure or someone helping out in the present moment; the rabbi also triggers associations from congregants' own past. At the same time, clergy need to pay attention to the private sources of their own feelings, so that they can discriminate past emotional residue from emotions and assumptions generated in present-day encounters. Rabbi Marcus's and Rabbi Stein's enhanced appreciation of transference/countertransference phenomena will sensitize them to their congregants' tendencies to admire and idealize persons of authority, as well as congregants' reluctance to express negative feelings. Clergy become the unassuming targets of a vast array of shifting emotional currents – anger, disappointment, cynicism, gratitude, love, and romantic yearning. Congregants may see the rabbi as a harsh, unavailable, or incompetent parent, or, conversely, an idealized or eroticized figure. The rabbi's reaction to this shifting tide of feelings (i.e. the rabbi's countertransference) must be monitored. The next vignette demonstrates how negative countertransference complicates the rabbi's response.

Example 4. A difficult congregant

Harvey and Rhonda Pullman, ages 48 and 47, and their three children have been members of the synagogue for over a dozen years. Since Shira Kane became rabbi seven years ago, Harvey has been someone she could count on to show up for a prayer service or lend a hand when needed. However, Rabbi Kane quickly came to realize that for every minute Harvey donates to the synagogue, she has to spend at least the same amount of time listening to his problems and complaints. While Harvey is punctilious and diligent, he is quick to get insulted and display his temper.

The past few years have not been kind to Harvey. His business and his marriage failed. Rhonda initiated separation, but they both live in the community. In two months, their youngest daughter will celebrate her ba mitzvah. Harvey challenges Rhonda on every detail. He drops by Rabbi Kane's office even more than before and sends numerous emails asking for advice and assistance. As if that weren't enough, Harvey and Rhonda's split has polarized the community. Multiple congregants contact Rabbi Kane. In addition to her involvement with Harvey and occasionally Rhonda, Rabbi Kane now has to field emails and phone calls from concerned congregants who register their opinions about how she should deal with them and the upcoming ba mitzvah. Rabbi Kane is sure that whatever she does will be deemed wrong.

Rabbi Kane appreciates Harvey's efforts to be helpful and feels sympathy for him. However, she also feels annoyed and exasperated. She catches herself trying to avoid encounters with Harvey. Her extensive efforts to help Harvey have not been rewarded. Now the community is looking over her shoulder and judging her. Rabbi Kane feels guilty about her negative feelings and her wishes to distance herself from Harvey. She thinks to herself, "My job as a rabbi is to be more patient and understanding."

Questions to consider

1. How do you know when to give a congregant extra attention or set limits?
2. What do you do when people in the community speak to you about other congregants?
3. How do you know when you are having negative feelings towards congregants?
4. What triggers negative feelings towards congregants for you?

Discussion

Rabbi Kane is struggling with negative countertransference. In earlier years, the rabbi felt that if she put in more effort, she could help Harvey change and manage better. Now she feels that her efforts to help this difficult congregant have backfired. Rabbi Kane feels disappointed in herself as she notices that she is avoiding contact with Harvey.

By recognizing her countertransference feelings, Rabbi Kane is able to step back, clarify her role, and make more deliberate choices in her interactions with Harvey and the community. Learning not to take Harvey's problems as her own personal responsibility helps Rabbi Kane clarify her interactions with Harvey, as well as with congregants who chime in with advice on matters involving the Pullman family. At the beginning of each call or meeting with Harvey, Rabbi Kane tells him how much time she has and sticks to whatever she sets up. The rabbi thanks people who express their concern for the Pullman situation and then explains that she does not discuss the family's situation out of respect for their privacy.

Every community has difficult congregants who take up a disproportionate amount of the rabbi's attention by challenging the rabbi's sense of doing a good job. Clergy have more difficulty recognizing positive countertransference reactions because it often feels good to be the object of this kind of transference. A type of positive transference that gets much attention is erotic transference. This term refers to the transferring of romantic and sexual feelings to the therapist or rabbi. Failing to identify erotic transference can have serious consequences and lead to boundary problems, as illustrated in the next example.

Example 5. Transference and countertransference between a college student and a Hillel rabbi

Aliza Golding drops by the Hillel rabbi's office frequently to chat and ask for advice. She admires 31-year-old Rabbi Jack Stein and loves seeing how sweet he is to his wife Miriam and their baby son. She contrasts him with her own father, who recently left her mother for another woman. Aliza hopes that she finds a boy-friend as nice as the rabbi.

From his side, Rabbi Stein, whose marriage is strained by a new baby with serious medical problems, finds himself looking for-ward a great deal to his chats with Aliza. He feels younger, freer, and more attractive when she is around.

Questions to consider

1. Is it wrong for clergy to feel attracted to congregants?
2. What do you do when you become aware that a congregant is attracted to you?
3. What do you do when you become aware that you are attracted to a congregant?

Discussion

The above situation is emotionally loaded and potentially combusti-ble. The degree to which Rabbi Stein is aware of countertransference feelings will be directly related to his ability to help Aliza. A lack of understanding can be catastrophic. The rabbi senses that he wants to spend more time with her and talk about his life. He also feels nerv-ous about how much he enjoys her company and wonders if he should avoid her.

Rabbi Stein should not avoid Aliza, because doing so might lead her to feel humiliated and abandon the Hillel setting. This would be an abandonment of his pastoral role. Her warm feelings represent a connection that should be directed in the service of her maturation and spirituality. Rabbi Stein should neither shut Aliza out nor flirt with her. Either behavior would deprive his congregant of needed support. Self-awareness enables Rabbi Stein to reflect and act purposefully rather than react. Just as he would with any student, Rabbi Stein chats with her in public spaces and during conventional hours. He encourages Aliza to join Hillel activities that are of interest to her and will help her broaden her circle of friends.

The next example illustrates how countertransference can interfere with the rabbi's availability.

Example 6. The rabbi retreats from a question

Rabbi Marcus and his wife Leah have been trying to conceive another child for several years and are under the care of an infertility specialist. At one of their appointments, they run into synagogue members Craig and Nina Gross in the waiting room. A few days later, Craig asks to meet with Rabbi Marcus.

Craig: Thanks for making time for me. You might not have heard, but Nina is three months pregnant. We had a really hard time conceiving. Since I saw you in the doctor's office, I realized that you and I might be struggling with the same issues.

Rabbi: What's on your mind, Craig?

Craig: Well, the doctor recommended that we use a sperm donor. Now I'm worried that I won't feel like the baby is really my own. Nina is so excited, but I'm feeling disconnected from the whole experience. I'm hoping you can give me some guidance because you probably have already thought about these kinds of things.

Questions to consider

1. How do you protect your personal privacy?
2. What do you do when you don't want to share personal experiences?

Discussion

Here Craig's transference stems from his belief that the rabbi will provide wise counsel to him. He assumes that since Rabbi and Leah Marcus struggle with infertility as he and Nina do, they will know how Craig feels. And, because he is a rabbi, Daniel Marcus will have the answers. Rabbi Marcus's immediate response to Craig's assumptions is complicated. As someone who continues to struggle with infertility, he cannot be fully objective in this matter. Further, Craig sought Rabbi Marcus out based on seeing him and his wife at the infertility doctor's office. While an encounter in a medical setting or other public space is to be expected in community life, for a congregant to act on such knowledge may lead the rabbi to feel that the congregant has invaded his privacy. Rabbi Marcus feels that Craig's call is inappropriate and invasive. Rabbi Marcus's awareness of his countertransference has two components. He realizes that the situation is too close to home for him to be the active, compassionate, non-judgmental listener that Craig deserves. In addition, he is aware of his irritation regarding the privacy violation. Rabbi Marcus's attunement enables him to explain that while he understands that Craig thinks they share an experience, Rabbi Marcus feels too caught up in the issue to be able to provide pastoral counsel. Rabbi Marcus tells Craig that his issues deserve a more objective listener and suggests alternate sources of pastoral support, such as other clergy in the synagogue or a rabbinic colleague familiar with issues of infertility.

Sometimes the goal of a pastoral encounter is for the rabbi to provide a highly circumscribed interaction before extracting him or herself from a pastoral role that is not appropriate. The pastoral principle here is that counseling needs to remain as neutral as possible. It is also possible that the nature of the transference/countertransference cannot or should not be worked through between rabbi and congregant, and so referral is in order. In the above example, Craig was looking for bonding and support. Although Rabbi Marcus might have been able to answer a technical question or respond to a more neutral request, he was not able to offer the level of personal connection that Craig sought and so tactfully referred him elsewhere. The question of whether it is helpful for clergy to share personal experiences will be discussed at length in Chapter 3.

In Example 4, the vignette of the college rabbi who is drawn to the student, Rabbi Stein works through his countertransference. Once he identifies the issue, he realizes that he can provide appropriate counseling to Aliza and others by adhering to counseling parameters and boundaries that we will detail in Chapter 4. In Example 6, the pastoral request based on an encounter in the fertility doctor's office, Rabbi Marcus's recognition of his countertransference prevents a pastoral relationship from becoming distorted or uncomfortable. An important component of pastoral counseling is identifying when to step back. A situation like Rabbi Marcus's, where personal reactions are likely to interfere with an optimal outcome for the congregant, is one such example.

When clergy struggle with an issue that is similar to the congregant's, they must evaluate their own feelings before deciding if they can be of help. The same is true of mental health professionals. Had Craig and his wife not run into Daniel and Leah Marcus at the fertility clinic, Rabbi Marcus might not harbor the countertransference component of feeling that his privacy was violated. Under different conditions, the rabbi might have been able to be more supportive. This further illustrates the importance of evaluating one's response to each and every encounter. A rabbi who has struggled with an issue very similar to that of the congregant, might, at a later point in time, when the rabbi has worked through and come to some resolution of the struggle, offer superb support and sophisticated resources. But for Rabbi Marcus to counsel Craig and his wife under the circumstances described provokes too many unresolved issues of his own and raises too many feelings for him to be helpful.

Notes

1 Rabbi Moses Isserles, known as the Rema, rules in Orach Chaim 27:1 that someone who does not have a left forearm should put *tefillin* on their left bicep but refrain from saying a blessing. Rabbi Israel Meir Kagan, known as the Biur Halacha, explains that other authorities rule in favor of such an individual making a blessing,

advising that the person can make both blessings when putting on the *tefillin* for the head, while having in mind that the blessing should count for the *tefillin* for the hand as well, thereby fulfilling the obligation according to all opinions. If the arm is amputated above the bicep, the Mishnah Berura 27:6 states that the individual is exempt from *tefillin* for the hand, though he quotes some opinions that rule that one should put the *tefillin* on the right arm but not say a blessing.

2   There are several different approaches found among Jewish legal arbiters regarding the prohibition of abortion. Rabbi Moshe Feinstein posits that it is included within the prohibition of murder (albeit not subject to the death penalty; see Shut Iggrot Moshe Choshen Mishpat 2:69). Rabbi Yosef Trani views the fetus as part of the woman's body and holds that abortion falls under the prohibition of causing self-harm (see Shut Maharit 1:97). Rabbi Yair Bacharach suggests that it could fall under the prohibition of wasting seed, i.e. masturbation; the intent seems to be that this prohibition includes any destroying of potential life (see Shut Chavot Yair 31). Rabbi Ben-Zion Uziel holds that there is an independent prohibition on destroying a potential Jewish life (see Shut Mishpetei Uziel 4:46). Rabbi Eliezer Waldenberg states that the prohibition on abortion is rabbinic, and not Biblical, in nature (see Shut Tzitz Eliezer 8:36). The approach one follows will affect the circumstances under which abortion could be permitted. If it falls under the prohibition of murder, it will never be permitted, short of saving the life of the mother. According to the other approaches, the threshold for allowing abortion would be lower. Justifying circumstances might include non-life-threatening danger to the mother (Mishpetei Uziel 4:46, Minchat Yitzchak, Likutei Teshuvot 138) or preventing the child from living a life of complete suffering, such as a child with Tay-Sachs (Tzitz Eliezer 13:102). We are not aware of any traditional authority who would permit abortion for financial inconvenience alone, although Rabbi Uziel does state that even a "weak reason" could suffice.

The gestational age of the fetus is a relevant factor as well, with some authorities distinguishing between the first, second, and third trimester in determining what would constitute justifying circumstances to permit an abortion (see Rav Ovadya Yosef, Shut Yabia Omer, vol. 4, Even Ha'Ezer 1, and Rabbi Waldenberg, Tzitz Eliezer, 13:102).

Regarding abortion prior to 40 days after conception, the threshold is significantly lower, and there are those who hold that there is no prohibition at all (Chavot Yair, 31; see also Breitowitz n.d.). Rabbi Moshe Feinstein (Shut Iggrot Moshe Choshen Mishpat 2:69) seems to indicate that there is no difference in the prohibition between before 40 days and after 40 days. However, several legal authorities hold that while there is still a prohibition before 40 days, it is of a lesser nature and could be permitted for lesser need than after 40 days (see Shut Tzitz Eliezer 7:48.1.8, Shut Achiezer 3:65). A competent legal authority with expertise in this area should be consulted before any such decisions are made.

For an overview of this topic, see Steinberg 2003, *s.v.* "Abortion."

References

Breitowitz, Yitzchok (n.d.). "The Preembryo in Halacha," www.jlaw.com/Articles/preemb.html, accessed June 30, 2016.

Nouwen, J. M. (1979). *The Wounded Healer: Ministry in Contemporary Society* (London: Darton, Longman and Todd).

Steinberg, Avraham (2003). *Encyclopedia of Jewish Medical Ethics* (Jerusalem: Feldheim).

Chapter 2

Pastoral counseling and mental health treatment

A comparison

A challenging area in pastoral care is the interface between pastoral counseling and mental health treatment. Even when the response to personal crisis includes clinical depression or anxiety, many people will seek out a rabbi because they wish to find meaning in times of transition or adversity. Mental health symptoms may require a different kind of intervention than a rabbi is prepared to provide. However, the rabbi is often in the front line and needs to address psychiatric problems, at least in their presenting stages.

Pastoral counselors need to be familiar with a wide range of psychological dynamics and presentations, as described in the previous chapter. In addition to enhancing the pastoral encounter, this knowledge helps differentiate between emotionally powerful reactions that fall under the domain of a pastor and those that are manifestations of clear psychiatric illness and require mental health treatment. When clergy encounter congregants suffering from disorientation as to time, place, or person, hallucinations, delusions, or marked changes in mood, this signals the need for mental health intervention. For example, a rabbi needs to recognize the differences between a normal grief reaction and pathological or prolonged bereavement that might require the attention of a mental health professional. Similarly, an educator needs to distinguish between extreme religious devotion and manic excitement or obsessive-compulsive disorder. This chapter outlines some of the differences between mental health treatment and pastoral counseling, such as:

- values
- scope of practice
- clinical boundaries.

Value-neutral versus religiously informed approach

Pastoral counseling and mental health treatment share significant principles and methodologies. However, there are major differences in their
underlying philosophies. First, each discipline approaches the meaning of human suffering from a different perspective. Psychiatrists, psy-
chologists, and social workers are trained to think of human distress
as a situation to be relieved. They identify signs and symptoms, make
diagnoses, and develop treatment plans. Religiously informed interventions also seek to relieve suffering, but see human distress as an
opportunity for spiritual growth and religious connection. Jewish pastoral counselors place life experience in the context of a historic and
religious tradition that encourages the search for meaning. While mental health practitioners value the search for meaning, their perspective
is generally guided by the personal history of the patient. A second
difference is that mental health providers approach patients from a
neutral perspective that does not favor an outcome based on a prede-
termined value system. For the psychotherapist, the patients' symptom
relief and increased wellbeing is the goal. A mental health provider
is likely to prioritize lifestyle decisions that decrease personal distress
and maximize happiness. In contrast, the rabbi's goals and responses
are significantly shaped by Jewish principles and ethics. When there is
a perceived conflict between Jewish tradition and personal happiness,
the rabbi may underscore traditional values above and beyond personal joy. For example, a rabbi might try harder than a psychotherapist
to preserve a marriage that keeps an unhappy couple together for the
sake of the children.

Congregants are often in pain because their feelings and behaviors do not conform to their religious code. A married Jewish woman
involved in an extramarital affair knows she has not only betrayed her
husband but has also violated a fundamental tenet of her faith. An
adult son who must make decisions regarding life support for a terminally ill parent may experience conflict between Jewish values that
advocate maximal sustaining of life and Western values that focus
more on quality of life and individual choice. Pastoral counseling hov-
ers in the middle space between arbitrating religious tradition and providing permission to explore personal feelings and thoughts. Clergy
support in mediating this space will impact congregants' immediate

decisions and influence their long-term relationship to Jewish commitment and tradition.

Unlike a psychotherapist, a rabbi may feel caught in an identity conflict between the roles of authoritative religious leader who represents a formal tradition with prescribed codes and that of a compassionate listener. Some issues, such as homosexuality, are particularly challenging for more observant individuals and communities, because Jewish religious law prohibits certain behaviors that are increasingly accepted in contemporary life. A pastoral approach assumes desire on the part of the congregant to remain connected to religious tradition. At the same time, maintaining fidelity to that tradition might restrict the type of solutions that clergy can offer.

Clergy are lamplighters and spiritual guides whose comfort and counsel is informed by religious wisdom as well as the principles of modern psychology. At the same time, many pastoral encounters include strategic interventions and practical suggestions. The next three vignettes illustrate pastoral counseling challenges where religious and secular values potentially collide.

Example 7. The spiritual life of children

Paul and Rina Miller, ages 34 and 33, are the parents of six-year-old twins. Soon after the birth of their children, the Millers joined the local JCC, where Ellen Shapiro, who holds a Ph.D. in Jewish Education, is the executive director and supervises educational programming. Rina took the lead in deciding to send the twins to the JCC's nursery school. Currently the family attends services on holidays and some Shabbat mornings. One day in mid-October, Rina calls Dr. Shapiro to discuss a 'quick question.' Dr. Shapiro sets a time to meet the next morning at the JCC after she drops the twins off at public school.

Dr. Shapiro: Hi, Rina. Good to see you.

Rina: Nice to be back at the nursery school again. I kind of miss those days. We certainly didn't have the problem then that we have now.

Dr. Shapiro: Oh?

Rina: Paul is all worked up about Halloween. You know that the twins are in first grade now in public school. Having a costume and going trick-or-treating is a big deal for kids. They want to do what the rest of their friends are doing. And it's fun!

Dr. Shapiro: Yes, Halloween is very popular.

Rina: Paul is really giving me a hard time with this. He keeps on saying that if we want to raise kids with strong Jewish identities, they can't do Halloween. It's a pagan holiday. Well, I went trick-or-treating, and no one can say that I'm not committed to Jewish values. While Paul will allow the kids to buy costumes now, he insists that they can only wear them on Purim.

Dr. Shapiro: That's an interesting idea.

Rina: I'm sure you're kidding about that, Ellen. You have kids. Telling six-year-olds in October that they have to wait half a year to dress up and have a big party is absurd. In fact, it's a great way for them to resent being Jewish.

Dr. Shapiro: Hmmm, so how can I help you, Rina?

Rina: I was hoping you would tell Paul to relax about Halloween and let the kids have a good time and go trick-or-treating.

Questions to consider

1. Should clergy intercede on behalf of one spouse in a family issue?
2. How do you feel about Jewish children participating in festivities that have become secularized but originate in other faith traditions?
3. Are you concerned about Jewish children feeling resentful or left out when they do not participate in secular festivities?
4. How would you reconcile parents who have divergent opinions?

Discussion

This brief pastoral counseling interaction featuring the "Halloween dilemma" presents interlocking challenges for the JCC director in terms of how to balance a religious agenda with family dynamics. While the encounter lasts only a few moments, it illustrates how pastoral preparedness enhances a casual conversation. Rina first asks that Dr. Shapiro endorse her minimalist perspective on the religious significance of trick-or-treating. Next, she places the JCC director in the position of allying with one congregant over another by requesting that Dr. Shapiro support Rina's view and not her husband's. This potential pastoral minefield requires tactful negotiation.

Dr. Shapiro has distinct ideas regarding young children and religious life. She understands that the early years are formative for the many sensory impressions and emotional experiences that form the bedrock of future religious life. She respects that cultivating the spiritual life of children requires just as much care and attention as does nurturing other aspects of developing minds and bodies. Knowing that small children learn best through activity and play, Dr. Shapiro works with the JCC's nursery school teachers to include age-appropriate Bible stories and preparation for Shabbat and holidays via food and decorations. She also believes that young children have an innate capacity for spiritual life. Her personal experience, along with her expertise in the psychology of early childhood, guides the philosophy and practice of the JCC's nursery school. Teachers talk to preschoolers and primary-school age children about God's presence in the world and teach them how to pray. This attitude also informs Dr. Shapiro's advice to parents of young children in situations of loss, such as divorce or death.

Dr. Shapiro strongly believes that Jewish identity is most powerfully transmitted through home practice and family education. From religious and cultural vantage points, she does not favor Jewish children participating in Halloween festivities. This aligns her with Paul's overall philosophy as to how to inculcate Jewish identity. At the same time, as an educator and spiritual leader, she realizes that she is likely to alienate Rina as a partner in future projects if she is perceived as siding with Paul. Dr. Shapiro decides to encourage Rina and Paul to downplay Halloween and be more pro-active about Jewish practices.

It would be a mistake for Dr. Shapiro to say something like, "Rina, I know you mean well, but Paul is right here. Wearing Halloween costumes and trick-or-treating are not appropriate activities for committed Jewish families." This sort of response would make Rina feel judged and like a less committed Jew than Paul. Rina would likely leave the meeting feeling diminished and reluctant to involve Dr. Shapiro in future issues. As JCC director, Dr. Shapiro is more likely to engage Rina if she can find a plane of empathy for her congregant's point of view. One possibility might be:

Dr. Shapiro: Rina, I'm glad you came to talk to me about this. I think that young children pick up on all kinds of messages that we send them. I like to see Jewish kids get excited about celebrating holidays. So to me this Halloween discussion is the beginning of a longer conversation between you and Paul about how to celebrate Jewish and other events and how you can compromise and cooperate to make this work in your family.

Rina: So are you saying that it's okay for the kids to do Halloween if we bring them more regularly to children's services or that we light Shabbat candles even when we go on vacation?

Dr. Shapiro: These are potential choices. But I think that you and Paul need to work this through together. What do you imagine he will say?

Both Rina and Paul want to be "right." Ellen Shapiro understands that each partner will seek validation from the spiritual authority. As JCC director who wants to engage with the Miller family for many years to come, Dr. Shapiro uses this encounter with Rina as an opportunity to solidify their relationship rather than solve an immediate problem.

Example 8. Reacting to interfaith marriage

Judah, the 23-year-old son of Don and Barbara Levine, one of Rabbi Marcus's most involved and supportive families, goes to London to study for a master's degree. Towards the very end of his year abroad, Judah writes a lengthy email to Rabbi Marcus describing how he has met the most amazing young woman at a Hillel event in London. Her name is Bonnie Solomon. Judah has never been so happy. He and Bonnie want to get married. He needs the rabbi's help because, although Bonnie's father is Jewish, her mother is Methodist. Judah writes: "Bonnie really feels good about her Jewish heritage, but I'm worried my parents won't accept her."

Rabbi Marcus writes back that he hears how happy Judah is, but that, yes, the situation is indeed complicated. He advises that they meet in person to talk about it more, when Judah returns to the U.S. in six weeks. Rabbi Marcus also asks when Judah plans on telling his parents about Bonnie, as he anticipates that once Don and Barbara find out, they will turn to him for help. Rabbi Marcus explains to Judah that as a rabbi to the whole family, he wants to be respectful of the confidentiality of each member. Three weeks later, Judah's parents call Rabbi Marcus and plead with him to counsel their son out of the relationship.

Questions to consider

1. What is your own position on interfaith marriage?
2. Should clergy put their efforts into breaking up an interfaith relationship or into engaging the interest of the non-Jewish partner in Judaism?
3. When there is family conflict, to whom does the rabbi owe allegiance?

Discussion

Rabbis are frequently in the position of counseling congregants who have fallen in love with someone whose religious status is problematic or who is not acceptable to all family members. As Rabbi Marcus parses the situation, he identifies several goals. His first priority is to maintain trust and goodwill among all members of the Levine family. Rabbi Marcus anticipates a certain amount of friction or outright collision within the family, some of which will be displaced onto him. He knows from past experience how distraught many parents become when an adult child announces involvement with a non-Jewish partner. Also, Rabbi Marcus seriously considers whether he has a responsibility to try and talk Judah out of proceeding towards a religiously compromised marriage. He certainly prefers that Judah marry a Jewish woman or that Bonnie convert. However, Rabbi Marcus wants to hold on to his relationship with Judah. He fears that counseling Judah to break up with Bonnie will alienate him from his family and his Jewish heritage and diminish the possibility of Bonnie going through a formal conversion process in the future. Rabbi Marcus faces a dual task. While he needs to help Judah think through the implications of a marriage that will cause some degree of religious marginalization, the rabbi also has a responsibility to Judah's parents, who are in crisis.

Early on in his conversation with Don and Barbara, Rabbi Marcus tells them that Judah had contacted him to share both his happiness and his great worry about his parents' reaction. The Levines are taken aback, "What, Rabbi? You knew this all along and didn't tell us?" Rabbi Marcus is prepared to answer, "Judah wrote to me a few weeks ago, and I knew you would hear about Bonnie very soon. It was important for me to respect your son's confidentiality. I felt it was up to Judah to give you his news. He was worried about your reaction. I'm glad this day is here, and we can now talk openly. I am the rabbi for all of you and I want to work with you as a family, honestly and together."

In a secular therapy situation, the goals in such a situation would be parsed differently. A therapist would query Judah as to whether he could live with the consequences of potential alienation from his tradition and family. The therapist would work within the value system espoused by the patient. This is similar to Example 3, in which Tova Rosen chose to consult her rabbi rather than a therapist about her unexpected pregnancy. A mental health professional would likely adopt a neutral stance and focus on Judah's stated goals. In contrast, Rabbi Marcus has a religious agenda that prioritizes exploring solutions guided by Jewish tradition.

In the situation of interfaith dating, the rabbi understands that contemporary young adult populations include a significant number of students with one Jewish parent. Their sense of religious and ethnic identity may not be correlated with the Jewish legal status of their mother or father. In many interfaith families, sensitive clergy can broker a solution that accommodates a common denominator. For instance, a woman who already feels Jewish may have less resistance to conversion if she feels accepted and respected.

Rabbi Marcus meets with Bonnie and Judah. He is impressed by the young woman's sincerity and commitment to Jewish life. However, Bonnie is reluctant to go through formal conversion because she feels that her mother will be insulted, as this represents a negation of her

Methodist heritage. The following summer, Judah calls the rabbi to announce that he and Bonnie expect to be married soon. In a subsequent conversation with the rabbi, Don and Barbara express disappointment but hope that Bonnie will convert in the future. Bonnie and Judah ask Rabbi Marcus to participate in their wedding. Rabbi Marcus examines his conscience and consults his own religious advisor. He informs the couple that while he wishes them well and looks forward to future involvement with them, he cannot participate in, or attend, their marriage ceremony.[1] When Judah and Bonnie express their disappointment, Rabbi Marcus does not challenge their feelings but explains that his own commitment to Jewish law necessitates choices that are sometimes difficult for him as well. Rabbi Marcus explains his decision to Don and Barbara in a separate conversation and helps them plan how to strategize their participation in the wedding.

The above example depicts the prominent role of religious commitment in shaping a pastoral intervention. Belief and tradition determine both Rabbi Marcus's choices and the boundary of his involvement. An additional consideration for Rabbi Marcus involves how his actions will be interpreted by other members of the congregation, as well as by his rabbinic peers. A reality of religious vocation is the political pressure imposed by contemporary denominational standards or community expectations. Ideally, the rabbi provides leadership based on his/her integrated wisdom, Jewish knowledge, and personal sensibilities. In practice, clergy, like other professionals embedded in vocations with high visibility and complex hierarchical infrastructure, must consider the consequences of their decisions in the larger political landscape.

Had Rabbi Marcus attempted to find a religious legal position that would allow him to participate in Judah and Bonnie's wedding, he would need to anticipate potential consequences. Although such considerations on the part of Rabbi Marcus would not come under the classic usage of countertransference, feelings of being criticized or being censured may be activated and interfere with what might be in the best interest of the individual congregant in a specific circumstance. Rabbinic responsibility includes consideration of how these larger sociopolitical issues affect individual congregants in need. This is accomplished by delineating clear boundaries of interaction and responsibility.

Example 9. A situation of death and burial that is not compatible with traditional Jewish law

Cindy Parker, age 22, became involved with Jewish life while at college. During her final semester, she makes an emergency visit to her parents' home in a distant city after learning that her mother's chronic illness has taken a dire turn. Cindy emails her Hillel rabbi, Jack Stein, for help.

Dear Rabbi Jack,
It looks like my mom only has a few days left, and the planning is up to me. She has insisted on being cremated after her death. I know this is not Jewish tradition, but as I feel I must respect her wish, I am wondering if you might guide me. Is there a proper way to spread ashes, or is there a certain amount of time I am supposed to wait before doing so? I have decided to hold a service in our backyard, one of my mom's favorite spots.

There is another issue. A few months ago, my mom went to the funeral of a family friend and was so moved by how the minister conducted that service. As the reality of her own death drew nearer, she told us that she would like that minister to lead her funeral. My dad and I were really uncomfortable with this and prevailed on her to change her mind. She agreed to have a rabbi lead her service but is adamant about cremation. I really don't begin to know how to find a rabbi to do this. I think my mom is going to die in the next day or two, and I know that Jewish custom is to have the funeral right away, so I want to be prepared.

Thanks for helping me out.

Questions to consider

1. How would you communicate with this young woman? Would you respond with email, text, or a phone call?
2. In the case where a violation of traditional Jewish law or custom crosses your red line, how do you maintain pastoral involvement?

3. Would you help a congregant find someone else to assist in a matter that you would not undertake yourself?

Discussion

Life-cycle moments, such as birth, marriage, and death, are nodal points that prompt greater connection to religious tradition. Rabbi Stein is touched that Cindy has turned to him as a representative of Jewish life and wisdom. He appreciates the dual burden that Cindy faces in wanting to honor her dying mother's request for cremation, while knowing that this goes against traditional Jewish law.[2] Rabbi Stein surmises that Cindy is committed to following her mother's wishes and that it will not be helpful to direct her efforts toward trying to change that decision. He focuses on Cindy's wish to maintain fidelity to Jewish religious tradition despite this challenge.

Given the emotional intensity and time demands of the deathbed situation, Rabbi Stein chooses to reply by email, so that Cindy can read the letter at her convenience and refer back to it. He addresses several points. He assures the young woman that the fact that her mother did not live a traditional Jewish life does not exclude Cindy and her family from meaningful aspects of Jewish practice. As cremation has not historically been an accepted Jewish practice, Rabbi Stein advises that, if possible, Cindy exempt herself from making those specific arrangements and instead direct her efforts towards creating a more traditional tone. These might include requesting that the ashes be buried in a cemetery, preferably a Jewish one, rather than keeping them in an urn in the house or spreading them outdoors. Rabbi Stein writes that, in the future, Cindy will note that other Jews visit their parents' graves, and she may wish to have a site to visit as well. Regarding the funeral service, Rabbi Jack suggests resources for finding a local rabbi, such as asking the funeral home. He also encourages Cindy to participate in Jewish mourning practices, such as delivering a eulogy, sitting *shiva*, and saying *kaddish*. He closes his email response with words of consolation and encouragement to contact him for any reason. Rabbi Stein marks his own calendar with a reminder to call Cindy three days later to see how the funeral went and then two weeks after that for follow-up.

Rabbi Stein has chosen to lessen Cindy's conflict about her mother's cremation by empowering her own Jewish practice. Another choice might be to take a more hardline position that emphasizes adherence to Jewish burial tradition. The risk of such an approach is causing Cindy to feel alienated from Jewish tradition and throwing her into greater conflict.

Examples 7, 8, and 9 illustrate religiously informed pastoral responses. While it is unlikely that any of these problems would have motivated the three congregants to seek mental health treatment, the issues raised might have been discussed in the context of an ongoing relationship with a therapist. These examples illustrate that while there is often rabbinic and therapeutic overlap, their domains differ. Neither Rina nor Judah nor Cindy sought counsel for problems associated with a mental health diagnosis. However, in dealing with congregants, clergy must be alert to presentations that require the kind of mental health intervention that is beyond the realm of pastoral care.

Knowing when to refer

While clergy stop short of treating mental illness, their frontline status offers them a unique perch from which to recognize distress. Clergy must be able to detect mental illness and be of support to mentally ill people and their families. An important component of pastoral counseling is to recognize when a situation is beyond the scope of clergy and requires an appropriate referral. A classic situation is in the case of depression, where the rabbi might be the first to notice a marked difference in a congregant's mood or behavior. We offer an example.

Example 10. Noticing a striking change in a congregant

Jane and Caleb Brown are members of Rabbi Marcus's synagogue. Jane gave birth to the couple's first child two months ago. The baby was circumcised in a joyous ceremony at which Rabbi Marcus officiated.

Before baby Saul was born, Jane regularly attended Shabbat services. Rabbi Marcus notices that she hasn't been back since giving birth. He assumes that she is home with the baby. The next time the rabbi sees Caleb in synagogue, he spends a bit more time asking about Jane and Saul. He notices that Caleb seems strained in his comments about Jane having a "hard time" adjusting to motherhood. Rabbi Marcus says that he and his wife Leah would like to drop by and visit Jane.

When Jane answers the door, it is obvious that the situation is not good. Jane appears to be a changed woman. She looks haggard and tense. During the visit, she repeatedly asks whether Leah thinks the baby is getting enough breast milk. When Rabbi Marcus inquires how Jane feels, she confesses that she isn't getting more than three hours of sleep a night and has already lost 25 pounds. Her own mother came for a week but then had to return home. Leah asks if Jane has ever felt this way. Jane replies that while she got nervous around big transitions in the past, it was never as bad as this. Rabbi Marcus knows Jane to be a highly competent woman. He feels very worried as Jane repeatedly states what a failure she is and how baby Saul deserves a better mother. Rabbi Marcus has met many new mothers and has some familiarity with typical "baby blues." He is also aware of the phenomenon of postpartum depression. Jane's words and demeanor lead him to wonder whether Jane is suffering from postpartum depression.

Questions to consider

1. How do you determine whether a congregant has a more serious mental health condition than you can handle?
2. How do you tell a congregant or family member that professional mental or physical health intervention is needed?

Discussion

Rabi Marcus's knowledge of postpartum depression helps him determine that Jane needs to see a psychiatrist immediately. Postpartum depression is a serious complication of pregnancy that generally responds well to medication and psychotherapy. Failure to identify and treat this condition can have serious consequences for the mother, the newborn, and the rest of the family. Rabbi Marcus understands that there are multiple safety concerns in this situation, such as suicidality.

Having confirmed his suspicion that Jane Brown's distress exceeds the "baby blues" characteristic of many new mothers, Rabbi Marcus's task is to make a referral. He explains to Jane and her husband that, based on his experience, Jane needs immediate mental health care. He urges the couple to discuss Jane's mood with her obstetrician. Alternatively, he can make a referral.

What is important is that Rabbi Marcus recognizes that Jane's situation warrants urgent care. He does not try to minimize, normalize, or ignore what he sees. He recognizes that it is beyond the scope of his role to try and treat this mental disorder. He will stay involved by checking in with Jane and Caleb through the resolution of her illness to provide pastoral support and to help mobilize community resources such as cooked meals or babysitting.

The next example is somewhat different, in that the congregant believes that she has a religious issue, while the rabbi detects an underlying mental health problem.

Example 11. Understanding scrupulosity

Lucy Barber, a 28-year-old radiologist, works at the medical center where Rabbi Shira Kane is the Jewish chaplain. Lucy and her husband have become progressively more interested in Jewish observance. Lucy attends Rabbi Kane's monthly medical ethics conference and occasionally attends Shabbat and holiday services with her husband. She has called Rabbi Kane multiple times with questions about keeping kosher. At first, Rabbi Kane commended Lucy's desire to be meticulously observant in this domain. Shortly before Passover, the volume of calls escalates. Rabbi Kane notes that Lucy asks the same questions over and over. She starts to wonder whether the young doctor's scrupulosity is in fact a question of religious zeal or alternatively a manifestation of obsessive-compulsive disorder.

Questions to consider

1. How do you distinguish between religious devotion and a mental health problem?
2. Should you assist someone in religious devotion if you detect underlying psychiatric illness?

Discussion

Obsessive-compulsive disorder (OCD) is a frequently occurring anxiety disorder. Because a person with OCD can function at a high level in circumscribed areas and because there are many seemingly positive aspects to being methodical and exacting, the disorder can go undetected for a long time. Indeed, people who suffer from OCD are exceedingly conscientious and have a strong work ethic that can serve them well in professions that require diligence and scrupulosity.

Religious observance, with its attention to detail, does not cause OCD but does provide fertile ground for the expression of obsessive thoughts and compulsive behaviors. Such behavior can be viewed as evidence of greater commitment and fervor. However, manifestations of OCD are not religious or spiritual expressions and should not be treated as such. The rabbi should be careful not to praise or inadvertently reinforce religious observance that seems overly intense, rigid, anguished, or belabored. Unusually repetitious behavior, particularly asking the same question multiple times or to multiple rabbis, often in the context of dietary or sexual issues, alerts the rabbi to direct the conversation towards an exploration of the congregant's larger psychological environment.

Rabbi Kane begins the meeting by letting Lucy know that she respects the young doctor's meticulous approach to observance and that she is there to assist her with any questions regarding Jewish law and practice. She next voices her concern that, in her opinion, Lucy appears more burdened by the details of observance than the spirit that the law requires. She gently inquires whether in other areas of her life Lucy is similarly preoccupied with details. Understanding that irrational fears often accompany OCD, Rabbi Kane probes as to whether Lucy worries about such untoward consequences of her actions. "Have you been bothered by thoughts that might not make sense, but still keep coming back into your mind even when you tried not to have them? Do you think that something bad will happen to you if you don't keep the laws exactly right?"

Rabbi Kane is attempting to determine whether Lucy's heightened attention to observance is part of a broader pattern of obsessions or compulsions that suggest OCD. If so, her task is to let Lucy know that the intensity of her scrupulosity may be interfering with her functioning. Referral to a mental health provider might help Lucy explore this further. Rabbi Kane would like to stay involved as her religious advisor. The suggestion must be made carefully because Lucy may feel hurt or insulted that her religious dedication is being interpreted as a mental problem. Rabbi Kane's offer to stay involved communicates that she is not trying to hand Lucy off, but rather help Lucy be a fully committed Jew.

Examples 10 and 11 demonstrate the importance of knowing enough about mental illness to detect its presence and make an appropriate referral. Clergy must cultivate a broad contact list of referrals. Referral is guided by the availability of local mental health practitioners and the congregant's preference. In Lucy's case, OCD is expressed via a religious ritual, and she might prefer a therapist who is also observant. Alternatively, she might feel more open and comfortable with a therapist who is completely outside the Jewish world but respectful of religious life. In either case, ongoing involvement by her rabbi will be invaluable throughout treatment and beyond.

Many psychiatric conditions remit and recur over time. Rabbi Kane's pastoral support will help Lucy understand and live with OCD and contextualize it along with her religious life. As there is a high risk of recurrence of postpartum depression, Rabbi Marcus will pay close attention to Jane Brown if or when she becomes pregnant again. He knows that hints of depression during pregnancy signal the need to deploy preventative strategies to try and ward off postpartum illness. Overall, clergy support lessens stigma and shame associated with psychiatric illness and encourages congregants to access needed care.

In addition to highlighting the importance of knowing how to identify major psychiatric conditions, the two examples above make an additional point about the difference between how clergy and mental health providers initiate care. In contrast to mental health sessions, for which people generally call to set up appointments, pastoral interviews come about in many ways. Congregants may contact clergy via phone or email to arrange meetings. However, they also bump into their rabbi after services, in the drug store, or at social functions, and then launch into discussions of all sorts. It becomes the rabbi's responsibility to shape these encounters in ways appropriate to the topic, the congregant's dignity, and the integrity of the rabbi's private time. If, at services or community events, the rabbi notices that a congregant looks different or upset, the rabbi goes over to check out that observation. Or, if the rabbi receives a call that a congregant has suffered a serious accident or medical emergency, the rabbi interrupts plans in order to contact the family and learn more about the situation. Depending on the circumstances, the rabbi might cancel plans and go to the emergency room to be with the family.

In yet another possible iteration, a concerned third party brings a pastoral concern to the rabbi's attention. Occasionally, a person will contact the rabbi to set up an interview for someone else, usually a family member or close friend. Unless the individual identified as needing pastoral intervention is not capable of initiating such a request, as in the case of a young child or a sick person, the rabbi does well to inquire why that individual is not making the call him- or herself. Generally speaking, it is preferable for a potential interviewee to contact the rabbi directly. Doing so establishes independent agency for the congregant and sets up a rapport more conducive to productive counseling. Sometimes, a congregant who calls on behalf of another person is reluctant to acknowledge his or her own need for rabbinic support and instead labels the other person as having the problem. Once again, active listening combined with sensitive questioning equips the rabbi to clarify the situation and make an appropriate intervention.

Initiation of pastoral care on the communal level, as well as in individual cases, constitutes another major difference between mental health and pastoral counseling. Clergy's response to individual or collective concerns also includes a variety of modalities that go beyond counseling. The next three vignettes show how pastoral counseling needs emerge in diverse situations and how clergy's repertoire of responses is similar to and different from that of other helping professions.

Example 12. Preparing for a bar mitzvah

Noah and Rochelle Blum ask Dr. Ellen Shapiro, the executive director and educational head of the JCC, to help prepare their 12-year-old son, Adam, for his bar mitzvah. The convention for boys in their community is to read the entire Torah portion, lead the morning service, and deliver a sermon. Rochelle and Noah explain to Dr. Shapiro that Adam, who has Asperger's syndrome and is in an inclusion class in school, wants to take on these commitments.

Three months into the project, Dr. Shapiro sees that the boy lacks sufficient proficiency in Hebrew language and other skills needed to accomplish his goal. Adam is demoralized and losing interest. He stumbles over words and shows up late to classes. During their final tutoring session, Dr. Shapiro has a heart-to-heart talk with Adam, who confesses that he is under too much pressure. The boy appeals to his teacher, "Please talk to my parents. They just don't get it that this is too much for me."

Dr. Shapiro calls Rochelle and Noah and invites them in for a meeting. She describes her perspective and suggests that they set more attainable goals for Noah. She explains that constructing a more positive experience will enhance his pride and connection to Jewish tradition.

Noah: Sure, I'm fine if Adam just does what he is comfortable with.

Rochelle: I can't believe you give in so easily. Adam is just lazy. He's perfectly capable of matching what Jeremy did at his bar mitzvah just three years ago.

Noah: Why can't you allow Adam to be who he is? He's done great, especially for a kid on the spectrum. Why do you always have to compare him to Jeremy?

Rochelle: Why do you always give up on Adam?

Noah turns to Dr. Shapiro and sighs. "You see how hard she drives everyone?"

Questions to consider

1. How do you transition to a pastoral counseling mode when you did not expect it?
2. How do you stay fair when a couple quarrel and both partners demand your loyalty?

Discussion

As an astute educator, Dr. Shapiro recognizes that she is witness to a longstanding marital pattern between Noah and Rochelle. She knows about Adam's diagnosis of Asperger's syndrome and over the years has worked with the JCC to make accommodations for him and other children with special needs. While she anticipated some pushback from the Blums in adjusting their expectations for Adam's bar mitzvah, Dr. Shapiro is surprised by how quickly the meeting turned to Noah and Rochelle's relationship. She assumes that these hints of marital friction regularly impact Adam and have implications for the rest of the family. This awareness allows Dr. Shapiro to transition smoothly into a more pastoral mode. Her task at this moment becomes strategizing between a focus on the format of Adam's upcoming bar mitzvah and the dynamics of Noah and Rochelle's marriage. She decides to put her initial effort towards deflecting tension over the bar mitzvah rather than addressing the marital strain.

As she listens and observes Noah and Rochelle argue, Dr. Shapiro feels worried for Adam, whom she identifies as her primary congregant for now. Adam is likely to feel humiliated by a poor performance and discomforted by his parents' quarreling. Dr. Shapiro is concerned that this combination might alienate him from Jewish tradition. Her goal is to bolster Adam's self-esteem and foster a positive religious experience. Dr. Shapiro understands that her success depends on authentic alliances with both Noah and Rochelle. She chooses her words carefully.

"The way I see it, Noah is not giving up on Adam. No one is giving up on Adam. I appreciate how you, Rochelle, value excellence. At the same time, my sense as a teacher is that Adam is under too much pressure. Even if we could ride him hard, I'm not sure the end product would be to his long-term advantage. My goal for a bar or bat mitzvah is to see the child grow up with a loving connection to Jewish tradition."

Aware that her response favors Noah's philosophy, Dr. Shapiro adds another comment that supports Rochelle's concerns.

"I agree with Rochelle that it's very important for Adam to feel pride in his bar mitzvah. We need to take into consideration that he knows what Jeremy did and will care about how his performance compares to that of his older brother."

Dr. Shapiro wants to model the importance of including Adam in significant decisions.

"For me, the chief goal of bar mitzvah is for the child to take on meaningful responsibility. How about if we ask Adam?"

As she anticipates, both parents retreat from her suggestion. Rochelle responds, "He'll just take the easy way out." Noah retorts, "That's just pressuring the kid even more."

Dr. Shapiro capitalizes on the fact that she has created a moment of alliance between the Blum parents in their joint resistance to her suggestion about involving Adam. She builds on their serendipitous cooperation with an educative point.

"I think that bar mitzvah is a celebration of a milestone. Each child should find his or her own way. Rather than put Adam in a situation of competing with his brother, how about if we find a way for him to uniquely experience his bar mitzvah?"

An additional tactic would be to refer to her accumulated wisdom and experience.

"I have seen many beautiful bar and bat mitzvahs where the child focused either on the prayer service or the Torah portion. I have also seen deeply moving celebrations where a child does a social action project. I strongly recommend that we give Adam some space so that he can create a positive and meaningful bar mitzvah for himself."

Dr. Shapiro hypothesizes to herself that part of Adam's negativity stems from the family dynamic. Children of couples in conflict express their own distress in a variety of ways. Some strive to be the perfect child in an attempt to patch up the family rift, while others, like Adam, function as a kind of wick for the tension at home. Dr. Shapiro is well aware that she has not been consulted as a marriage counselor. At the same time, her role as a Jewish educator invokes religious authority. Dr. Shapiro feels an obligation to at least note what she observes. In this setting, she might address the situation in a general way that connects to the upcoming occasion.

"Milestone events can be very positive and exciting times in a family's life, but they also can cause some tense moments. How about we focus on the bar mitzvah for now? During the next 12 months as we work together, you'll all have time to think about whether this tension is specific to this event or whether you think it is more general and deserves extra attention."

If, during the ongoing bar mitzvah preparation, Noah and Rochelle start talking more and more about tensions in their marriage, Dr. Shapiro should not take on the work of being their couples counselor because that is not her mandate. Even if the rabbi or educator has professional training in this field, conducting ongoing marital therapy conflicts with the communal, social domain of clergy. Dr. Ellen Shapiro will be far more helpful by remaining available as a religious and educational resource person for the Blum family and, if needed, making a thoughtful referral for Noah and Rochelle to a marriage counselor.

Clergy play critical roles when tragedy strikes and affects the larger community. In such situations, their pastoral role spans individual and collective concerns. The next story describes a pastoral response following a sudden death.

Example 13. Aftermath of a sudden death on campus

Three days before the Chanukah ball on campus, Jared Glazer, a 20-year-old college junior affiliated with Hillel, dies in a fall from his dorm roof. It is not clear whether Jared was under the influence of drugs or alcohol or whether his death was a planned suicide. The news spreads quickly through campus.

On hearing of the tragedy, Rabbi Jack Stein texts Jared's roommate, Roy, to check in about how he is feeling and to see if he would like to arrange to speak. Roy texts back immediately that he needs to talk. Though it is now 10 p.m., Rabbi Stein agrees to meet him in the Hillel office right away. Roy is distraught. He tells Rabbi Jack that he was not aware of Jared having any particular difficulties. The rabbi listens quietly to the young man's outpouring of guilt and self-incrimination. Roy also speaks of his need to do something useful in response to Jared's death but does not know what that should be.

After several minutes Rabbi Stein intervenes. He assures Roy that this type of tragedy is not a result of his failure to notice a problem or do the right thing. They talk for another half-hour and decide that it would be helpful to establish a Facebook page where friends and others who knew Jared could share their feelings and memories. Information about funeral arrangements and *shiva* could also be posted there. People trickle into the Hillel lounge throughout the night and into the next day. Rabbi Stein and other Hillel staff rotate to sit with students through the night as they express their shock and grief. Later that day, a few hours before the Sabbath, arrangements are made to transport Jared's body to his hometown for burial.

Rabbi Stein decides that Shabbat services are an appropriate place to address the community's trauma. He meets with the students who lead services to discuss how to handle the challenge of responding to the community and also respecting Jared's privacy. The rabbi also considers the tradition of not holding public mourning on the Sabbath.[3] He suggests that students acknowledge Jared's untimely death and add some appropriate psalms but mostly stick to the regular Shabbat service. Students also discuss mixed feelings about whether to have the gala Chanukah ball as planned.

Questions to consider

1. What has been your experience with community trauma?
2. What interventions have you seen help people?
3. What interventions have you seen that do more harm than good?
4. How far should life "go on" after a community tragedy?

Discussion

When trauma and catastrophe strike a community, people need some form of public response to help metabolize the powerful feelings of fear and grief that are evoked. While natural disasters, random violence, and suicide each carry a different emotional valence, pastoral presence can provide enormous support during ensuing emotional turbulence. The actual tasks of the rabbi and Hillel staff described above are not radically different from those deployed by a mental health provider at the university. However, the typical mental health provider might not have taken Rabbi Stein's first step of figuring out who Jared's roommate is and establishing an initial communication. Furthermore, conventional mental health resources would not offer a natural way to link student mental health concerns at this time with social and religious events such as Sabbath services and the Chanukah ball.

In this situation, Hillel staff might collaborate with mental health resources available through the university in order to combat the copycat phenomenon that comes up in the wake of suicide in teens and young adults. For example, given that the tragedy occurred to a member of the Jewish community, the rabbi might ask campus mental health services to provide a suicide prevention program at the Hillel. A substance abuse program could similarly be implemented. Pastoral presence helps reassure vulnerable persons that the appropriate staff is ready to help them deal with ideas of self-harm through talking and exploring emotions, rather than by acting on impulses that could be deadly.

In the above example, the Hillel rabbi functioned as a pastoral grief counselor following the death of a known member of the college community. Clergy must also respond to distant traumas, such as crises in Israel. They need to decide how to break painful news to children of different ages in camps and schools, as well as whether to continue with planned celebrations. Further, as members of the community, clergy must deal with mental health issues in ways that mental health professionals would not. In the next two examples, we consider pastoral responses to public displays of psychiatric illness.

Example 14. Mental disorder and recovery: public or private?

In Rabbi Marcus's synagogue, congregants deliver the Saturday morning sermon once a month. Isaac Stone, a 56-year-old married marketing consultant who is a serious, quiet person, sends Rabbi Marcus the following sermon that he would like to deliver:

> Today's Torah portion describes a group of people that dwell outside of the camp so that they do not contaminate the others. The rabbis discuss the primary cause of their illness as slander, speaking ill of someone, an act that is considered spiritually impure. Interestingly, the Torah does not discuss

the plague from the perspective of the afflicted person. One of today's plagues is mental illness. Six per cent of the U.S. population suffers from a serious mental illness. They and those close to them feel stigmatized and worry that someone will speak ill of them or consider them defective.

Therefore, I want to speak a bit about my life and my road to recovery. Most of you do not know this, but I have bipolar illness. I struggle with this, and it is often a source of shame. My symptoms started with severe depression as I struggled with major work projects that I was unprepared for. I wished I had never been born or I pictured my car losing control and plunging into the lake I passed by on my way to work. Untreated, one out of five people living with bipolar illness commits suicide. My mania was probably triggered when, as a senior executive, I had to lay off several employees. I didn't know what to say to my co-workers, and they didn't know what to say to me. I kept my illness locked up in a dark closet, trying to hide it from most of my family and co-workers

Thank God, things turned around with a new job and a change in medication. I became involved in a small support group for people with my illness. I realized that I am not alone, and if you are struggling with mental illness, you too are not alone.

Questions to consider

1. What is your reaction to this proposed sermon?
2. Is it advisable for someone in recovery to go public with a personal experience?
3. What reactions would you anticipate from your community if you decide to go ahead with the congregant delivering such a sermon?

Discussion

As Rabbi Marcus reads Isaac's sermon, he is deeply moved by his congregant's struggle, honesty, and commitment. He wonders how the community will respond to these disclosures. He also wonders what impact delivering the sermon will have on Isaac. The rabbi knows of several other members of the community who have had mental health challenges and felt stigmatized by them. He thinks that openness and public dialogue will help relieve the burden of shame carried by so many, including people who have not revealed their problems to him. At the same time, Rabbi Marcus feels concern as to whether it is a good idea for Isaac to go forward at the present time and deliver this sermon. In considering whether to give Isaac the pulpit for his sermon, Rabbi Marcus notes that the piece is well organized, clear, and insightful. This indicates to him that Isaac is stabilized in his recovery. Still, just as the rabbi would be wary about a congregant running a marathon soon after a physical injury, he feels cautious about Isaac's putting his psychiatric history in the public spotlight.

Rabbi Marcus meets with Isaac to discuss the overall matter and his concerns. He asks Isaac what his wife and his psychiatrist think about him delivering the sermon. If all agree that it is okay for Isaac to go ahead with the sermon, Rabbi Marcus will agree to it. Rabbi Marcus will meet with him before the sermon slot to provide support. The rabbi will also meet with Isaac afterwards to check out how the experience felt for him. Rabbi Marcus anticipates that members of the congregation will feel mixed emotions. Some might experience relief, knowing that they are not the only ones living with psychiatric illness. Others will feel scared, put off, or moved to start telling their own stories. The rabbi needs to be especially alert to this last reaction. Isaac's sermon is not intended as a springboard into making Shabbat morning a group therapy or encounter session. Rabbi Marcus must be prepared to tactfully contain and redirect spontaneous revelations from other congregants that he determines are inappropriate for the setting. This likely involves making himself available to meet with congregants who are especially moved by Isaac's words.

If Rabbi Marcus decides that delivering the sermon is not a good idea right now, he needs to help Isaac find another way to honor his insights and feelings about his illness and mental health in general. This might include planning the talk for a smaller venue, giving it at a later date, or publishing it in the synagogue newsletter.

The next story is similar in that it deals with a mentally ill community member, but one who has chronic illness and poor insight.

Example 15. The limits of tolerance

One Saturday morning, an unfamiliar middle-aged woman appears in Rabbi Marcus's synagogue. She is messy-looking, with uncombed hair, oddly applied make-up, and layers of wrinkled clothing. The rabbi notices people moving away from her. She stands at the wrong times, prays loudly and fervently, and seems unaware of others' discomfort. At kiddush, she eats ravenously. Rabbi Marcus walks over to greet her. She introduces herself, "Hi Rabbi, my name is Sabine. It's so nice that you came over to me. I'm hungry. Can I come to your house for lunch?"

Questions to consider

1. How do you balance inclusivity towards eccentric people and communal discomfort with odd behaviors?
2. How do you manage unstable people who transgress basic standards of communal conduct?
3. Can you make treatment adherence a condition for participation in communal activities?

Discussion

Rabbi Marcus believes that the synagogue should be a place of prayer, learning, and community for all Jews. In addition to serving mainstream congregants, he tries to cultivate a welcoming, friendly atmosphere that is comfortable for marginalized people who seek material and spiritual services and social connection. He is proud that his synagogue sponsors a food pantry and clothing drive and provides festive meals for individuals who do not have families with whom to celebrate holidays. At the same time, Rabbi Marcus recognizes his responsibility for the safety and wellbeing of the entire community. While he wants the synagogue to be a welcoming place, it is not a mental health treatment facility. Rabbi Marcus knows that unknown and odd-looking individuals will evoke discomfort and possibly fear in the people around them. He knows that if an individual is psychotic, meaning that he or she is not grounded in reality, that person might be prone to unpredictable and possibly dangerous behaviors.

Rabbi Marcus takes the lead in modeling hospitality tempered with caution. He understands that a crowded kiddush room is not the place to attempt an interview. He also does not feel comfortable inviting Sabine, about whom he knows nothing but whom he suspects may have some form of chronic mental illness, to his home. Rabbi Marcus's goals at this point are to ascertain that Sabine has shelter, give her a package of food, and set a time for her to return to the synagogue so that he can get to know her and her situation. He responds to her request, "I'm very happy to meet you, Sabine. Today is not a good day to invite you over, but I certainly can see to it that you get some food to take home for lunch. By the way, where is home for you? I'm also wondering if you could come back to the synagogue on Monday or Tuesday so we can get acquainted better."

Sabine shows up at the synagogue on Monday and asks to see the rabbi. During their meeting, Rabbi Marcus finds out that she has moved back with her elderly parents, Izzie and Gloria Feldman, who live across town. Sabine is vague and withholding about a past history of "being in hospitals." She starts to attend the synagogue regularly and joins the weekly Bible class. Her behavior in class is disruptive – she brings multiple shopping-bags and dominates the discussion with insistent, abrasive questions. Rabbi Marcus notices that other congregants avoid sitting near her. Class attendance drops over the subsequent weeks.

While Rabbi Marcus is committed to his synagogue being open to all Jews, including those with conditions that are unattractive, he is concerned with people feeling so uncomfortable that they leave. Further, he does not think that Sabine is getting much benefit by causing distress in the various environments she enters. Rabbi Marcus wants to meet her parents to get more information about her. He asks Sabine for permission to do so, and she refuses. He considers whether calling her parents anyway could be considered a breach of confidentiality but decides that in her state, she may not have adequate capacity to make a decision in her best interest.

Rabbi Marcus calls Sabine's parents. Izzie and Gloria Feldman are quite frail and unwilling to intervene in any way. Sabine has gone missing for months at a time but lives with them now. They are relieved that she is under their roof and eating decent food. Gloria Feldman reports that Sabine received psychiatric care in the past, carries a diagnosis of schizophrenia, and has been prescribed various medications. She and her husband are not sure what, if anything, their daughter is taking at the present time. They politely decline any intervention from local mental health support services. The phone call confirms Rabbi Marcus's hunch that Sabine has chronic mental illness. He also recognizes that while her parents are concerned about her, they are overwhelmed and are unlikely to be active partners in their daughter's care.

Rabbi Marcus meets with synagogue staff. Together they establish basic guidelines for Sabine's behavior so that she will not disrupt activities or annoy others. These include limiting her to a single shopping-bag in the synagogue and one or two comments per class. Rabbi Marcus and a female staff member explain all this to Sabine after class and she reluctantly agrees.

A seemingly calm month goes by. Then, Rabbi Marcus receives a long, ranting email from Sabine in which she accuses another member of the Bible class of having deliberately poisoned her food and plotting to do even more terrible things. Sabine writes, "I have no other recourse than to protect myself and other members of this synagogue. I plan on telling everyone I can about that woman's evil intentions and defending myself."

Consistent with the course of her illness in an untreated state, Sabine has suffered an acute relapse. Last year Rabbi Marcus attended a continuing rabbinic education seminar that outlined basic facts about severe psychiatric disorders. He remembers that he should not challenge her paranoid delusions or attempt an intervention other than guiding her towards treatment. He calls a psychologist colleague at Jewish Family Services and explains the situation. The psychologist agrees to evaluate Sabine and arrange for medication if necessary. Next, Rabbi Marcus asks Sabine to come in for a daytime meeting. He checks with building staff that able-bodied synagogue employees are nearby and available in case Sabine loses control and they need to contain her before emergency services arrive.

Rabbi Marcus tells Sabine that he is concerned about her health and wants her to go for a consultation. Sabine retorts, "Rabbi, you just don't believe what I said about that woman poisoning me. You are taking her side." Rabbi Marcus does not attempt to refute her comment. He simply states, "I haven't heard of anyone else getting ill from the food." Sabine counters, "Rabbi, so you think I'm nuts, don't you?" Rabbi Marcus responds calmly, "I can see that you are upset and suffering. I want to help you get the treatment that you need to feel better. I can help you set up an appointment with the doctor at Jewish Family Services. You need to do that in order to come to class and services here."

The challenge here is balancing Sabine's need for religious and social support with the safety and comfort of the synagogue community. Rabbi Marcus knows that schizophrenia is a relapsing disorder that often renders people isolated. While chronic mental patients are rarely violent, their bizarre mannerisms alienate most people around them. Medications that treat their acute symptoms also cause numerous side-effects. This leads to widespread non-adherence and diminished capacity to work or participate in other conventional social activities. Religious institutions such as synagogues, community centers, and schools share an ethical responsibility to include such members. At the same time, clergy and lay leaders serve the broad membership and must address concerns such as creating an attractive environment and ensuring safety. One of Rabbi Marcus's goals in the above vignette is to get an assessment from a mental health professional that will guide his approach to Sabine and her involvement in the synagogue community.

Rabbis, educators, and communal leaders occupy powerful positions in terms of educating the larger community and exercising leverage over congregants with erratic control of their mental illness. Such people respond best to clear, consistent directions that guide them as to whether certain behaviors are acceptable or unacceptable. Clergy may also deputize other congregants to help support this effort, as in the example with Sabine. Just as volunteers visit the sick and organize activities, so too congregants might welcome isolated persons and sit with them during services. Physical presence exerts a powerful calming influence on a person who lacks self-regulation. Just as Rabbi Marcus checks in advance that synagogue employees are in the building before his meeting with Sabine, he also asks several congregants to take turns keeping her company at community events.

The examples in this chapter highlight the interface between mental health and pastoral counseling to underscore the unique religious dimensions of pastoral care. Another area where pastoral roles are distinct is their understanding of borders and boundaries. In the next section, we describe the nature and limits of pastoral boundaries.

Firm borders versus flexible boundaries

Mental health work develops most effectively when therapist and patient have no contact outside of the therapeutic relationship. Consider how a psychologist designs the practice to remain relatively anonymous to patients. The psychologist meets patients in an office setting and avoids social contact with them outside the professional space. The patient contacts the psychologist to initiate contact and pays a fee for each session. This standard operating procedure cannot apply to clergy, who forge multilayered pastoral relationships within community. A rabbi lives and works in the same community as his/her congregants. The rabbi meets with congregants at their request and also reaches out to them to initiate pastoral visits. Unlike the psychologist, the rabbi often conducts sessions in places other than the office and does not charge for pastoral counseling services.

The rabbi serves not only as pastoral counselor but also as religious role model, ritual director, wise advisor, teacher, spiritual counselor, and community organizer. These multiple roles create broad webs of relationships with congregants and influence the rabbi's attitude toward boundary regulation. In contrast, the therapist is singularly focused on providing assistance for circumscribed problems for which the patient has sought care. The rabbi's many spheres of interaction have the positive consequence of reducing stigma often associated with seeking mental health treatment. Scheduling an appointment with a therapist may feel like an admission that there is a major problem, while going to the rabbi can more comfortably be viewed as seeking counsel from a wise person.

Because clergy are so visible in the community, their personal lives are more widely known and they have a range of relationships with congregants. As the rabbi's pastoral identity is not easily disconnected from the rest of his or her life, it can be very challenging to maintain boundaries. Maintaining boundaries is a central tenet in mental health treatment and, as described above, is facilitated by specific protocols and practices. In the absence of the well-delineated professional guidelines that govern mental health practice, the rabbi needs to create a specific context for pastoral counseling so that it is differentiated from other rabbinic activities. This also protects the rabbi from feeling on-call at all times to congregants and allows the rabbi to try to go home at the end of the day in a similar way to a mental health professional.

Boundary crossings

For the reasons described above, pastoral boundaries are difficult to establish, confusing to negotiate, and easy to transgress. The terms "boundary crossings" and "boundary violations" help distinguish between unusual behaviors that are acceptable and those that wander across conventional lines and veer into danger (Gutheil and Gabbard 1993). In this lexicon, boundary crossing refers to a bending of protocol, a discrete piece of behavior that may be unconventional but is essentially benign and may even be helpful. A useful rule in determining whether a behavior constitutes a boundary crossing or a violation is to ask if the practitioner would try to keep it a secret.

Examples of appropriate boundary crossings for clergy might include:

1. A college student calls the rabbi in distress, and the rabbi accompanies him to an emergency room at midnight.
2. A JCC director takes an isolated widower to buy new clothes.
3. A chaplain telephones the estranged daughter of a nursing home resident and persuades her to pay a visit to her dying mother.

While none of these activities is typical or routine, each could reasonably be viewed as appropriate to clergy's pastoral role. Neither the rabbi, nor the JCC director, nor the chaplain would feel the need to keep their activities clandestine; these are boundary crossings, not violations. Recall Rabbi Marcus's visit to Jane Brown, the new mother suffering from postpartum depression, in Example 10. A typical mental health worker would not be likely to make such a bold and intrusive visit. Such an intervention, however, is necessary to help Jane to seek the kind of mental health care she needs. Note that Rabbi Marcus plans his intervention with boundary awareness in mind. He makes the decision to invite his wife when he realizes that the situation warrants a home visit to a female congregant. He wants to avoid any ambiguous interpretation on the part of the congregant or anyone who may learn of his visit. Had Leah not been available, the rabbi would have made sure to bring another person or to time the visit when Caleb, Jane's husband, was at home.

Boundary violations

Boundary violations are harmful, exploitative, or repetitive behaviors that a person would be loath to have known to others. Such violations often begin with small boundary crossings. Again, if a rabbi feels that some activity he or she has with a congregant is better kept secret, that rabbi is on the verge of a boundary violation. When clergy fail to recognize and manage inevitable transference/countertransference feelings, minor boundary crossings risk growing into frank violations.

Example 16. Accepting an invitation from a congregant

Juliette Krauss, a 35-year old member of the synagogue, calls Rabbi Marcus, an avid music fan, and asks him to accompany her to a cello and piano concert that her friend cannot attend. Juliette is friendly with Leah Marcus and knows that she does not like chamber music. Rabbi Marcus politely declines her invitation. However, when she offers him both tickets, he accepts them and pays their cost.

Questions to consider

1. Under what conditions do you socialize with congregants?
2. What standards should apply to rabbis, educators, and other spiritual leaders when it comes to socializing with congregants?

Discussion

Juliette does not mean her invitation to be romantic, and Rabbi Marcus does not perceive any such motivation. However, he understands that the situation is fraught with complexity. Even if he pays his way and accompanies Juliette, he considers the implications of being seen in public with a woman who is not his wife. He is also concerned about the date-like setting and the potential for kindling romantic feelings in either of them. If Juliette had several extra tickets and Rabbi Marcus was included in a larger group, this might be different. In contrast, a therapist should neither accompany a patient to the concert nor accept and pay for both tickets. The parameters of the therapeutic contract preclude such social interchange. Clergy, on the other hand, regularly navigate between personal and communal spheres.

The terms "boundary crossing" and "boundary violation" are not limited to the highly publicized sexual transgressions most often enacted by male clergy, but rather include many areas of conduct that apply to clergy of both genders. In fact, having too narrow a definition of boundary issues might prevent clergy from paying attention to early hints of trouble in areas such as influence and money. It is important to keep in mind that a rabbi's unique position renders the rabbi privy to congregants' deepest feelings and most closely guarded secrets. The volatile mix of a congregant's trust coupled with the rabbi's own temperament and personal situation can trigger feelings of special understanding and closeness. It is also very tempting to assume that the more intimate the connection with a congregant is, the more far-reaching and transformative the rabbinic relationship will be. However, efforts that are "special" and depart from convention are more likely to be a set-up for boundary blurring that invites transgression. Once again, the rabbi must pay attention to his or her emotional pulse and note when a reaction departs from the rabbi's conventional pastoral baseline. The next example illustrates a boundary challenge that touches on a different kind of intimacy.

Example 17. Responding to an inappropriate request

A recently married academic couple in their late thirties learn that they are infertile. Their reproductive physician tells them that an egg donor would be a good option, but that there is a shortage of eggs from Jewish women, which is their first preference.[4] The couple approach Rabbi Jack Stein and ask for his help in fulfilling a mitzvah. As he knows many female Jewish undergraduate and graduate students, they hope that Rabbi Jack would inquire if some might consider egg donation. They assume that the rabbi will be especially motivated to help because he supports their wish to have a family.

Questions to consider

1. How do you feel about helping this couple with their request?
2. How do you communicate your boundaries when you feel that a congregant request is over the line?

Discussion

Rabbi Stein feels sadness for the couple's plight and understands their desire for a baby. He thinks they would make wonderful parents, and indeed, he is acquainted with many Jewish women in their twenties in the university community. Some of them might even see helping this couple achieve their dream of building a family as a great act of kindness. Anyone would appreciate the generous sum that the couple is willing to pay. However, the rabbi also recognizes that the situation is rife with pitfalls. While Rabbi Stein supports the couple in their quest to build a family, he deems their request as inappropriate because he cannot use his position to solicit eggs from young women who are congregants of the university community. The procurement of genetic material is an intimate and complicated activity. Rabbi Stein explains his concerns to the couple and refers them to an infertility support organization that will counsel them on how to advertise for egg donors or achieve adoption through conventional channels.

The romantic or physical realms are most often thought of in relation to clergy transgressions, but attunement to other boundaries is also important. Other controversial situations may involve money or other misguided invocations of influence.

- A key officer threatens to quit a day school board if the principal refuses to drop a health education program that advocates safe sex practices.
- A wealthy congregant suggests that the rabbi's support in a contentious custody dispute will garner significant financial gain for the synagogue's building fund.

Such situations hover on the border of manipulation. They demand both diplomatic skill and also ethical clarity. Ethical dilemmas require explanation. Outright extortion requires a firm statement of policy. Clergy may try to appease opposing parties and negotiate conflict. They must be prepared, however, to forfeit money or prestige if compromising their principles is expected as part of the bargain.

One of the differences between a rabbi and a mental health professional is that it is possible to negotiate a boundary in a rabbinic relationship that would not enter a conventional relationship with a mental health professional. For example, clergy may choose to play sports or do other recreational activities with congregants. For the rabbi to be on the same softball team as congregants does not merit exceptional attention. Taking a shower after the game in the same locker room, however, verges on the inappropriate.

Sexual misconduct, a most notorious violation, often starts with small deviations from conventional behavior in a climate of unacknowledged attraction between rabbi and congregant. Sexual activity between clergy and congregants is usually fostered by earlier breaches of protocol, as described in the following story.

Example 18. The slippery slope of sexual boundary violation

Carly Axelrod, an adult female congregant, asks her rabbi for help with a difficult marital situation. She requests that they meet early in the morning at the synagogue in order not to jeopardize her job. The rabbi obliges with several sessions scheduled after morning services but before the synagogue office staff arrive. Carly begins to call and email the rabbi to update him on her situation. The rabbi feels drawn to her plight and flattered by her appreciation. She begins to text outside of conventional hours, usually late at night. The rabbi, who feels a special connection with this congregant, replies within minutes. He starts to confide his own marital woes. One morning, as they get up to leave, Carly pulls the rabbi into an embrace and kisses him.

Questions to consider

1. How do you establish meeting protocols?
2. How much should clergy share their own personal struggles?
3. How much have you shared your own story and challenges?
4. What do you do when boundaries are crossed?

Discussion

This vignette is rife with boundary violations. While the congregant in this story is the active seducer, clergy always bear the prime responsibility for maintaining clear boundaries. The rabbi in this story ignores multiple warning signs of transference/countertransference complications. Instead of affirming protocol with respect to time and place, he colludes with Carly in transgressing conventional boundaries by holding appointments and communicating at unusual times. The intimacy generated further blurs the pastoral gradient and encourages the rabbi to divulge his own problems. This in turn prepares the scene for a further transgression, namely a physical expression of sexual attraction.

We suggest a question to help determine in which category a behavior falls. Simply ask yourself, "How would you feel if someone found out about what happened between you and your congregant?" If your answer is: "This may be a little unusual, but I have a good explanation," the behavior is most likely a boundary crossing that you can reasonably justify. It might be useful for you to check in with a colleague. On the other hand, if your answer is, "I wouldn't want anyone to find out," you are likely to be treading in the danger zone of a boundary violation.

Sexual misconduct by clergy violates an interconnected series of secular and sacred boundaries. The religious codes that regulate conduct with the opposite sex create an effective safeguard for these issues. An offending rabbi, who may at the same time be a charismatic leader and gifted teacher, breaches core religious and ethical values. In doing so, the rabbi abuses the sacred privilege of authority and causes profound harm to victims and to the community. Media attention is likely to follow and cause further damage to the reputation of individual clergy and religious institutions. The same is true, albeit with less publicity, of financial misconduct. The powerful emotional and spiritual connections that are often present in vibrant pastoral counseling offer infinite opportunities for boundary crossings and violations. The premise going forward ought not to be what to do *if* unexpected, intense, and possibly erotic feelings develop between clergy and congregant. Clergy must expect that such feelings are bound to occur and be prepared to respond appropriately *when* such situations occur. Clergy must establish policies that safeguard against boundary violations. In partnership with lay leadership, they must create respectful reporting protocols in synagogues, schools, camps, and other institutions. Clergy must be prepared with resources to turn to when boundary problems arise. This list includes religious and psychological mentors, legal guidance, and appropriate disciplinary protocols established by professional clergy organizations (Friedman 2009).

Chapters 1 and 2 explored pastoral counseling in broad strokes and addressed similarities and differences between pastoral counseling and mental health treatment. These include underlying values and responses to people's needs. Like therapists, clergy practice active, compassionate, non-judgmental listening attuned to transference and countertransference nuances. Clergy, however, subscribe to a value system based on religious tradition. As pastoral counseling is more closely defined by religious values than is mental health, the scope of its work is more expansive. Clergy's multiple relationships with a community lead to greater involvement and access. This requires understanding the limits of pastoral care and also keen awareness of boundaries and borders with respect to personal participation. In the next chapter, we detail concrete aspects of developing pastoral presence and conducting a pastoral interview.

Notes

1 Officiating at or participating in an intermarriage is prohibited according to Jewish law. Because intermarriage is forbidden, such participation would constitute assisting or enabling a transgression (*"lifnei iver"* and *"misayeia li'dei ovrei aveira"*). Attending as a guest is primarily a policy question of whether the rabbi's presence will be seen as condoning the intermarriage. Some legal authorities advocate for more lenient conversion policies in the case of a child of Jewish descent who is not Jewish according to Jewish law, such as the child of a Jewish father and non-Jewish mother (a concept referred to as *"zerah Yisrael,"* or "Jewish stock"). Absent such a conversion, however, the marriage is still considered an intermarriage.
2 There is no specific prohibition on cremation *per se*, but there is an affirmative responsibility to bury a dead body (see Shulchan Aruch Yoreh Deah 362:1), and cremation would be prohibited as an abrogation of this responsibility. A child is forbidden to listen to her parents if they tell her to violate or not fulfill a mitzvah or even a rabbinic obligation (see Shulkhan Arukh Yoreh Deah 240:15, based on Bava Metzia 32a and Yevamot 5b). Regarding burial, Shulchan Aruch Yoreh Deah 348:3 rules that even if someone instructs that he does not wish to be buried, his wishes are to be ignored, and he is to be buried regardless.
3 Public displays of mourning on Shabbat are prohibited (see Shulchan Aruch Yoreh Deah 400:1).
4 There is a debate among legal authorities regarding whether the genetic mother or the gestational mother is the legal mother. Using a Jewish egg donor would prevent any questions about the child's Jewishness (see Birkner 2010; "In-Vitro Fertilization," in Steinberg 2003; "Egg Donation," *The Couple's Guide to Jewish Fertility Challenges*; "Egg Donation," *Nishmat*).

References

Birkner, Gabrielle (2010). "Fertility Treatment Gets More Complicated," *Wall Street Journal*, May 14.

"Egg Donation," in *The Couple's Guide to Jewish Fertility Challenges*, www.jewishfer-tility.org/egg-donation.php, accessed June 30, 2016.

"Egg Donation," *Nishmat*, www.yoatzot.org/article.php?id=112, accessed June 30, 2016.

Friedman, Michelle (2009). "Crossing the Line: What Makes a Rabbi Violate Sexual Boundaries – And What Can be Done about It?" in *Tempest in the Temple: Jewish Communities and Child Sex Scandals*, ed. Amy Neustein (Waltham: Brandeis University Press), pp. 43–59.

Gutheil, Thomas G. and Glen O. Gabbard (1993). "The Concept of Boundaries in Clinical Practices: Theoretical and Risk-Management Dimensions," *American Journal of Psychiatry* 150: 188–196.

Steinberg, Avraham (2003). *Encyclopedia of Jewish Medical Ethics* (Jerusalem: Feldheim).

Chapter 3

Pastoral presence and personal life

Pastoral visits occur by design or spontaneously and take place in diverse settings. The goal of this chapter is to help clergy be attuned to nuances that impact on their effectiveness. Rabbis need to be aware that their behavior both on and off duty will be keenly scrutinized. The rabbinate is not a nine to five job; it is a vocation. Asking "Is this what a rabbi does? Is this what a rabbi says? Is this how a rabbi looks?" helps maintain awareness of that vocation. These parameters of behavior demonstrate that each and every communication contributes to the pastoral encounter.

What's in a name?

How clergy and congregant address each other influences the pastoral encounter. In considering what title the rabbi prefers and how the rabbi addresses congregants, the rabbi needs to consider the uneven gradient between clergy and congregant. These decisions go a long way in communicating the borders and boundaries of the rabbinic encounter. One of the complications of selecting a preferred title is that the rabbi may not want to use the same title for all people and in all settings. The formality implied in using the title "rabbi" feels respectful to many people, just as the use of "doctor" conveys deference to the doctor's expertise and competence in medicine. Doctors may not use their title in social situations because it describes them in a certain context that is limited to their function in a medical capacity. However, a rabbi is always a rabbi. At the same time, a tinge of "outsider-ness" comes with the title "rabbi" because it sets the rabbi apart. While there are times that this "outsider-ness" is appropriate and helpful, there will be other times that being addressed as "rabbi" feels lonely. Someone may interrupt an off-color joke or quiet a boisterous conversation when the rabbi unsuspectingly walks over.

Thus, clergy need to spend time thinking how they want to be addressed, by whom, and under what circumstances. How do rabbis indicate their choice of title and name? With the mental health professional, there is usually a moment of introduction at which time the therapist is in charge of this decision. A psychologist might say, "Hello, I'm Dr. Kline," "Hello, I'm Dr. Margaret Kline," "Hello, I'm Margaret Kline," or "Hello, I'm Margaret." Encounters between therapist and patient are relatively predictable, since they take place in professional spaces and at designated times. Encounters with clergy are not as formal or demarcated. The moment when the rabbi is introduced to a congregation or organization creates an opportunity for the rabbi to indicate what he or she wishes to be called. Subsequent rabbi–congregant encounters offer new naming opportunities. When Rabbi Daniel Marcus is meeting with the newly bereaved Green family to discuss the funeral for Matthew Green's 87-year-old mother, he is likely to introduce himself to out-of-town relatives as "Rabbi Marcus." On the other hand, if he is sliding into second base at the synagogue softball game, does he expect his congregants to shout "Run to third, Rabbi, run!" or "Run to third, Daniel, run!"? Similarly, whether a Hillel rabbi introduces himself to a freshman or to the university provost as "Rabbi Stein," "Rabbi Jack," "Rabbi," or just plain "Jack" will shape his rabbinate.

Congregants will make their own choices as to what to call their rabbi. Many clergy, especially in school, college, or hospital settings, feel that first name usage imparts warmth and availability. First names evoke easy familiarity and de-emphasize the sense of rabbinic "otherness." At the same time, the level social playing field suggested by first name usage might diminish the rabbi's impact as an authority figure or mentor. Clergy need to decide whether consistency of title is important to them. Do different people in the congregation call the rabbi by different names? What meaning might this have for different congregants? Do the ages of rabbis and congregants in any given situation play into these decisions? It might be helpful for clergy to consider how they want relatives and old friends to address them. For example, if the rabbi's first cousin or college friend comes for a visit, do they use the title "rabbi" in public?

Sometimes a congregant's choice of address feels uncomfortable or inappropriate. Recall Example 12, the story of the parents quarreling about their expectations for their son's bar mitzvah. Noah and Rochelle Blum customarily call the educational director, Dr. Ellen Shapiro, by her first name. If, during a heated discussion, one of them were to call her "Dr. Shapiro," that choice could indicate a wish for authority, or, alternatively, disdain for her advice. Similarly, Rabbi Jack Stein, who serves on a college campus, introduces himself as "Rabbi Jack." If a student switched to the more formal "Rabbi Stein," that would be meaningful. Context and tone changes help clergy decode potential meanings in the shifts used in title or name. Using the same logic, an uninvited casual address may come across as disrespectful or too familiar. In either case, clergy need to choose whether to acquiesce to or correct an appellation with which they are not comfortable. A brief vignette illustrates.

Example 19. Handling a change in title

Rabbi Marcus meets with Don and Barbara Levine the day after their son Judah has told them about his involvement with Bonnie, the young woman he fell in love with while spending a semester abroad and whose mother is not Jewish. This story began back in Example 8.

Barbara: Rabbi, Don and I are devastated about this situation. You have got to help him and us. I beg you, please do anything to convince Judah that this relationship must end.

Rabbi: I understand that this comes as a huge shock to you.

Don: What I can't get over, Rabbi, is that you have known about this for a few weeks. Honestly Daniel, isn't this your job? To make sure that Jews do the right thing? How could you not tell us that you knew about Judah and Bonnie?

Questions to consider

1. Why has Don switched from "Rabbi" to "Daniel?"
2. If you were Daniel Marcus, would you comment on this change?

Discussion

Emotions run high in this encounter between congregants and rabbi. Barbara's first response is distress coupled with a wish that the rabbi, like a powerful parent, can fix the situation. Don's reaction is anger. He has supported Rabbi Marcus and now feels betrayed. His switch signals a shift from the more respectful title of "rabbi" to the casual, even scornful, way he would address a peer who failed him. Rabbi Marcus's pastoral attunement enables him to note Don's switch from addressing him as "Rabbi" to "Daniel." While a therapist would explicitly point out a similar shift in titles in order to mine the underlying emotions, Rabbi Marcus does not take this route. While he understands that powerful feelings fuel the encounter, his mandate is to guide Don and Barbara rather than interpret their motivations.

The counterpart choice of how a rabbi addresses congregants has meaning. Some rabbis feel that calling adult congregants by their first names is disrespectful. Others take their lead from congregants' preferences.

The following pointers can guide you as you formulate your own protocol.

- What is your preference for what your congregants call you?
- Do you want to be addressed differently in different settings?
- Can different people address you differently in the same setting?
- Under what circumstances would you correct a congregant's choice?
- How do you choose whether to address congregants by their first or last names or titles?

A rabbi's choice of how to be called goes in tandem with his/her use of language. In speaking and writing, clergy not only impart information and ideas but also demonstrate that important Jewish values, such as respect and privacy, are embedded in communication. Clergy should also be thoughtful regarding use of slang and commonly used vulgarities. Coarse language in speech or writing may imply casual, loose behavior and be interpreted as an invitation to breach other boundaries. Overly formal language, on the other hand, may come across as pompous or unapproachable. A positive alliance is established by tone of voice as well as content. Again, what works for one rabbi may not feel right for another. Gentle, short, yet clear comments or questions such as "You seem concerned" or "Would you like to share your thoughts with me?" help establish a pastoral encounter. "Thank you for your trust" and "It was good to talk" acknowledge appreciation of meaningful conversation.

Social media expand the realm of clergy communication. Rabbis, educators, and lay leaders must assume that whatever they write on blogs, Facebook, Twitter and any other portals will be forwarded onward. Their words or photos are likely to be cut and pasted in ways that alter or even twist writers' original intentions. Consequently, use of social media demands ongoing evaluation of its impact and the responsibility of clergy to monitor communication streams.

In addition to what a rabbi says and how the rabbi says it, clergy must pay attention to appearance, as described below.

Rabbinic visibility

In the context of this discussion, visibility refers to the rabbi's grooming, clothing, and behavior. Personal habits and the rabbi's own notion of his or her role contributes to choices regarding appearance and wardrobe. For example, a man who gave little care to his grooming in his younger years might not be attentive to regular shaves or haircuts. However, a rabbi who is shabby or unkempt compromises his ability to garner full respect. All clergy do well to keep in mind that people want to feel that their rabbi, like their doctor, is conscientious, thoughtful, and stable.

The clothing worn by a hospital chaplain or campus rabbi is likely to be different than that of a rabbi who heads an urban synagogue. Extremes of either trendy fashion or very casual clothing may not be appropriate to the public rabbinic role. While clergy deserve to enjoy expressing individual taste, their grooming and clothing should be in keeping with community standards of modesty and the values that the rabbi wishes to impart to the community. This includes the cost of garments and accessories. Wearing an expensive gold watch, even one that is inherited, carries different valences of meaning to different people. For example, it may be difficult to convince congregants to shift to a less opulent standard of celebration when the rabbi wears a solid gold watch or costly designer clothing during the week. Similarly, it is more difficult to impress on congregants the need to support the synagogue if the rabbi displays personal wealth.

Congregants pay closer attention to and talk more about what women rabbis wear.

Female clergy's clothing is scrutinized for being short, tight, or revealing. Further, women clergy's private lives become public fodder when they gain or lose weight and certainly when they are visibly pregnant. Along with celebrating the joyous life event of expecting a child, some congregants are discomforted by the undeniable evidence of a female Jewish spiritual leader having a sexual life. Others may worry whether the rabbi will have time for them once she has a new baby of her own to care for.

Clergy understandably may chafe at the thought of curtailing personal style and self-expression. When does the rabbi get to relax? When Rabbi Daniel Marcus plays shortstop at the synagogue softball game and gets upset with the umpire's call, does he have the right to express his dissatisfaction loudly, perhaps with a few colorful words thrown in, like everyone else? Will Rabbi Shira Kane be labeled sloppy for showing up to the grocery store in a sweatshirt or provocative for wearing a fitted, sequined dress to the hospital gala? Will students or faculty deem it inappropriate for Rabbi Jack Stein to work out in the university gym and sit in the steam room afterwards? This kind of scrutiny can feel stifling for clergy and breed resentment that leads to burnout.

The overarching point is that rabbis are always rabbis. When doctors leave their offices and take off their white coats, they go about their private lives. In contrast, rabbis are always seen as representing their vocation. A few stories highlight the need for clergy to be mindful of the degree of scrutiny with which their personal decisions will be met.

Example 20. What to wear to the beach?

Rabbi Shira Kane is invited with her family to a large Sunday afternoon summer party at the beach home of a board member. Many members of the synagogue will be there. The invitation specifies that the activities include a barbeque and swimming. Rabbi Kane loves ocean swimming and rarely gets a chance to spend time at the beach.

Questions to consider

1. Would you wear a bathing suit in front of your congregants?
2. Should Rabbi Kane's husband and children wear bathing suits at the party?

Discussion

Mental health professionals avoid this conundrum by not accepting invitations to patients' parties. Clergy, however, regularly attend social events and need to consider that their clothing has implications. If Rabbi Kane wears professional clothing to the barbeque, she will dampen the relaxed atmosphere. On the hand, wearing a bathing suit may be uncomfortable for her and the other guests. If Rabbi Kane wants to swim in the ocean, she might consider going before the party or in a more private part of the beach. At the party she selects a casual outfit that suits the mood.

With regard to her family, in this situation, Rabbi Kane's husband and children represent the rabbi and so dress modestly as well. When the Kane family goes to the beach on a private vacation, they dress according to their personal standards.

Example 21. A different school for the rabbi's child

Rabbi Jack Stein and his wife Miriam debate whether to enroll their three-year-old son Gabriel in the local *Chabad* nursery or the Jewish Community Center (JCC) community pre-school for the fall. On Shabbat afternoon soon before school begins in September, Miriam runs into Maggie Lawrence, a faculty member and the mother of one of Gabriel's playmates from the secular toddler group both children attended the previous year. Maggie expresses her dismay that Gabriel is not continuing with the community pre-school at the JCC along with her daughter. "I guess we felt kind of sideswiped – as though the community pre-school isn't good enough for you ... like pluralism is okay to talk about on campus, but when it comes to your own kid, you don't want him in too open an environment ..."

Questions to consider

1. Do you feel compelled to explain personal decisions to congregants?
2. When is it acceptable to say, "I'm sorry, this is a private matter"?

Discussion

The Steins' decision to send Gabriel to the *Chabad* pre-school reflects a number of issues related to their son's needs and their religious philosophy. While choice of school is a private matter, it often becomes a topic of community discussion when it comes to clergy's children. Congregants will interpret school choice as an index of the rabbi's true philosophical allegiance. Some congregants take pride when rabbis' children attend more religiously conservative schools; others feel that such a decision renders the rabbi and the rabbi's family out of touch with or dismissive of their concerns.

As the rabbi's spouse, Miriam is cast into a clergy role by Maggie's confrontation. At first Miriam feels resentment that her and Jack's private decision about their child's schooling is public property. Miriam thinks carefully before she responds. She realizes that she has a pastoral obligation to share her reasoning. "We would really like to have a pre-school run by the synagogue. Part of the reason that Jack and I came here was to build the kind of community that expresses our values. I hope that in a few years we'll have our own pre-school. Until then, I'm not perfectly comfortable with the *Chabad* nursery, but I'm not altogether in sync with the JCC either. I guess each of us has to do our best until we build the right school together."

Personal choices such as where clergy send children to school might be considered a private matter. But taking that stance is difficult for a public person and is particularly difficult for the local rabbi. While the rabbi and the rabbi's family do not have to defend personal decisions, they can leverage such inquiries to deepen discussion on matters of community concern. People see the rabbi as a role model and might want to understand his/her decisions because they want to understand if they are making the right decisions for themselves. Thus, while some congregants' questions arise out of a desire to be inappropriately intrusive or challenge the rabbi, other inquiries come from a place of congregants challenging themselves.

Example 22. The rabbi's daughter gets in trouble

Rabbi Kane's 15-year-old daughter Sophie, along with several classmates, is implicated in cheating on a chemistry exam. Soon after the incident comes to light, the rabbi and her husband Max attend a parent program at the community high school that focuses on academic integrity. As they find seats, a congregant in the row behind them whose child was also involved in the cheating incident whispers loudly to his wife, "I was so shocked to hear that Sophie is a cheater. I guess we all expect that the rabbi's daughter would know better."

Questions to consider

1. How has public scrutiny affected your expectations of your children?
2. How do you respond when your child behaves imperfectly?
3. Do you owe your congregants any explanation for your child's missteps?

Discussion

Some of the lessons learned in the previous chapter serve the rabbi well here. Rabbi Kane's attunement to her countertransference is essential. Criticism of the rabbi or her family, whether direct or whispered, is bound to raise strong feelings of anger, anxiety, and shame. The rabbi needs to take care that her response to her child is not over-determined by other people's reactions. She keeps in mind that the whispering congregant is avoiding his own disappointment and anger at his child's cheating by focusing on the rabbi's family as failed role models. At the same time, Rabbi Kane must be aware of the impact of public scrutiny on Sophie. Neither the rabbi nor her husband needs to respond in the moment to the other parent. Both need to attend to what is going on with their daughter.

Clergy and their families are not immune to rocky relationships and difficult situations with their own parents, siblings, spouses, and children. Unlike the rest of the community, their trials and tribulations are watched more closely as evidence of the success or failure of religious life in navigating marriage, parenthood, and life in general. When Rabbi Shira and Max Kane found out about the cheating scandal, they were very upset. They asked themselves if they put too much pressure on Sophie or, the opposite, neglected her needs. Their first order of business was to discuss the situation with their daughter to determine her reaction. This includes whether she is remorseful and whether the cheating is a sign of a brewing rebellion. Either way, Rabbi Kane's attention is on her daughter. In this incident, she is a private person and does not have a pastoral obligation. At the same time, Rabbi Kane's reaction to Sophie may serve as a model for other parents with their own children. Just like every other parent, Rabbi Shira and Max Kane attend the program to learn how to better transmit ethical and academic values. This also sends the message to their children and to the rest of the community that they, just like everyone else, struggle with contemporary problems.

People thinking of following religious vocations do not often consider the restrictions and awareness demanded by the clergy role. Clergy must acknowledge and work through feelings of restriction or frustration generated by these constraints. People look to clergy as models for how to translate ethical and spiritual values into real life. This imposes a burden on clergy and their families. The story of Sophie Kane in Example 22 demonstrates how clergy parents need to avoid being overly harsh and not reprimand their children due to shame or pressure. In addition, rabbis need to find private arenas of self-expression and relaxation. They deserve to unwind and have fun. Relaxing in town with other clergy who share similar experiences or enjoying the company of old friends are potential times of ease. Personal outlets might be engaging in hobbies or recreational activities. Self-awareness and self-care are critical to the health and vitality of clergy and their families. We suggest some basic pointers:

• Keep in mind that people look to you and your family as role models.
• Seek out colleagues or friends outside the community that you can confide in.
• Find opportunities to relax and unwind.

We now turn our attention to the private realm of clergy and their families. The physical, psychological, and spiritual wellbeing of the rabbi as well as that of the rabbi's spouse and children form the cornerstone of successful pastoral counseling. In this section we address unique challenges faced by the rabbi and his or her family. These include privacy, loneliness, and the need for support.

Privacy for the rabbi

The fact that the rabbi, the rabbi's family, and congregants are all members of the same community can make it feel that life is lived in a fishbowl. In Example 6, Rabbi Daniel and Leah Marcus's visit to the fertility doctor was not treated by their congregant as private or off-limits. In fact, he sought to use this knowledge to improve his own situation. Similarly, in Example 22, where Rabbi Shira Kane's daughter cheated in chemistry, the rabbi felt the brunt of congregants' idealized expectations and subsequent disappointment. The sense that the community's eyes are always on the rabbi can lead to feelings of exposure, loneliness, and otherness.

Concern for public reputation can deter the rabbi from asking for needed support and counsel in times of trouble. Such isolation can result in burnout or boundary infractions. In Example 5, Rabbi Jack Stein might have decided that deepening a private friendship with Aliza Golding, the college student, would be enjoyable for both of them. This would be a dangerous boundary crossing. It is tempting for the rabbi to be drawn into a relationship in which the rabbi is perceived as a regular man or woman rather than as a rabbi. While the rabbi must attend to self-care, it is hazardous if the rabbi inadvertently or deliberately seeks to fulfill personal needs via pastoral counseling relationships. This is more of an occupational hazard for clergy than therapists because of the all-encompassing role of rabbi in the community compared to the more circumscribed role of the mental health professional. Thus, while the rabbi is friendly with congregants, the rabbi cannot expect to be best friends with them. The rabbi does not confide personal problems to congregants. When roles do become blurred in appropriate ways, such as if a single rabbi and congregant want to date, the rabbi is responsible for considering the effect of such involvement.

An added complexity is that the nature of meaningful religious engagement requires clergy to connect psychologically and spiritually with congregants, even those who do not actively solicit contact. In contrast to mental health professionals who avoid social contact with patients, rabbis have regular and deliberate emotionally charged interactions with congregants in a wide variety of social settings. In fact, congregants may experience their most meaningful religious moments in informal encounters such as sharing a festive meal with the rabbi and the rabbi's family, singing together at a community gathering, or working late into the evening on a charity project. Clergy regularly enter a situation expecting one kind of interaction only to find that their expression of concern elicits a whole new set of issues and needs.

- The rabbi inquires about a congregant's sister-in-law at Shabbat dinner and suddenly is hearing the details of a complicated family feud.
- An educator checks in with a student whose grades have slipped and becomes the confidante of the student's crisis of faith.

Further, in order to be effective religious leaders and pastoral counselors, rabbis must be equally available to all members. They need to be tuned in to perceptions of favoritism on all levels, whether social, financial, political, intellectual, or spiritual. Naturally, clergy will be more drawn to some people than others. Part of the pastoral counseling skill set is regular identification of "bright spots" and "blind spots," namely, the specific personalities and issues that trigger the rabbi to draw closer or avoid certain congregants. Figuring this out enables the rabbi to offer equal pastoral access to all congregants. This applies to social invitations, goods and services, and personal relationships. For example:

- Lay members of the congregation issue invitations to festive meals at their home to whomever they choose.
- The rabbi and his/her spouse are careful to rotate their invitation list throughout the entire congregation.

Larger celebrations pose related challenges.

- When congregants plan a child's wedding, they invite selected friends and family. Clergy and spouses are usually included on the guest list as a courtesy.

- When the rabbi's child gets married, either everyone or no one from the community is invited.
- When the rabbi has a personal birthday party, the rabbi invites only family and friends from outside the community.

These dynamics wend their way into clergy's seeming non-professional life. For example, clergy frequently join groups in which their membership has no clergy function but is nevertheless invoked.

- Dr. Ellen Shapiro is one of the sixth-grade parents at the local day school. She feels people staring at her when her son is rambunctious at a middle school event, and she senses their unspoken criticism.
- Rabbi Daniel Marcus plays shortstop on a local softball team. He is asked to intone a victory prayer before a game.

Clergy need to recognize that as leaders of congregations or communities, they are always set apart. The rabbi is never just another one of the people in the room. He or she is the rabbi. This concept is difficult for seminary students and novice rabbis as they anticipate forging relationships with congregants as friends, peers, and revered elders. The rabbi is not alone in this. Politicians and celebrities share these same issues.

- Do you have close friends who are also congregants?
- Can you ever just be a private citizen in the community?
- To whom do you go to for support and supervision?

These are all questions that frequently arise in clergy's vocational life. A related topic is how clergy manage personal information.

Managing personal information and disclosures

In contrast to the therapist, who does not professionally interact with friends and neighbors, clergy life is lived in full view of the community. A certain portion of the rabbi's personal life is bound to be public information. Congregants often know a great deal about the rabbi's personal history, interests, and family. They know about the failed effort to publish a novel, the struggle with a medical condition, and the child with a severe stutter. Such material brings up issues and feelings for all. Earlier in this book, when comparing pastoral counseling and mental health treatment, we discussed how the availability of information impacts transferences to the rabbi in contrast to the therapist.

People are naturally curious about the rabbi's personal life and divulge facts and rumors. In a situation where the congregant knows accurate information, rabbi and congregant may feel that discussion of shared experiences enhances their conversation. The rabbi may feel that since a congregant already knows that he or she has faced comparable challenges, it is okay and even helpful to share specifics for the purpose of navigating the congregant through similar waters. However, detailed knowledge of the rabbi's private struggles rarely benefits the congregant. In fact, such information is likely to distract from the congregant's issues and diminish the pastoral purpose by burdening the congregant with the need to respond to the rabbi's dilemma. Though the instinct to reveal personal history may be motivated by the desire to normalize human difficulty and form a common bond around shared experience, the long-term health of the clergy–congregant relationship is better served by keeping details private. Even if aspects of clergy's personal life are known, counseling sessions are neither the time nor the place to divulge extensive information about a past struggle with gambling, a brother's schizophrenia, or an elderly parent's decline. While clergy may feel that personal disclosures would facilitate the pastoral alliance, details of the rabbi's life are more likely to lessen congregant's motivation to discuss his or her own troubles.

Some congregants may pull for such disclosures, believing that mutual sharing of experiences makes them special. However, this type of relationship allows congregants to avoid dealing with their own issues because they are caught up in taking care of the rabbi. Some may resent that such disclosures detract from the focus on their own issues. For example, a disgruntled congregant reports to a friend, "I can't believe it. I went to the rabbi to talk about my mother's dementia, and he went on and on about his mother's problems with Parkinson's!" While the rabbi may have referred to his mother's situation only in passing, and with the intention to demonstrate empathy for his congregant's plight, this deflection from the issue at hand was not helpful. In general, a person struggling with an acute problem does not appreciate hearing similar tales of woe experienced by others. Another mistake is when the rabbi attempts to provide per-spective by pointing out that, in the scheme of things, the problem is not so bad. The rabbi may offer a story in which a similar situation had a much more terrible outcome. For example, in responding to a mother's complaint that her daughter breaks her 11 p.m. curfew, the rabbi should not respond, "Consider yourself lucky. When my sister was that age, she didn't come home until dawn!" One of the biggest problems with disclosure is the assumption that superficially similar experiences carry the same emotional valence and affect people in the same way.

Example 23. The rabbi makes a *shiva* visit

Rabbi Kane, whose beloved father died a few years ago, pays a *shiva* call to Roger Schwartz, a congregant whose recently deceased mother was a neglectful parent. Not knowing this his-tory, the rabbi opens her visit by saying, "I know how sad you feel. I lost my father three years ago, and I miss him every day." The congregant stiffens. An awkward, tense visit ensures.

Questions to consider

1. What assumptions do you tend to make about common life-cycle experiences?
2. How does your listening make room for congregants to express feelings that diverge from the norm?

Discussion

Clergy should never presume to know how someone feels. While per-sonal experience informs pastoral wisdom, it should not determine or limit pastoral imagination. In the above scenario Rabbi Kane might simply have said, "I'm sorry for your loss" and sat quietly to wait for the congregant to speak. If the *shiva* conversation seems banal or off topic, the rabbi might insert a simple question like, "I didn't know your mother. Might you tell me about her?" If Roger avoids a direct response to such an invitation, the rabbi does not pursue further inquiry. On the other hand, if Roger starts to express anger towards his mother or relief about the death, the rabbi's job is to listen and offer supportive words such as, "It sounds like you had a hard relationship with your mother."

Material about a clergy's past that is not public is best kept private. For example, high school students have little to gain in finding out whether their rabbi failed calculus or smoked marijuana as a teen. A far better use of discussion time would be to explore how different answers to such questions might relate to the students in the here and now. For some, knowing that their rabbi was a lackluster student and experimented with drugs might minimize the potential problems of such behavior. Others might view the rabbi's trajectory out of the teen years as an inspiring example of the potential for changing course. And, for yet other students, a rabbi who never tried pot might be seen as naïve. While clergy's private experiences hopefully enlarge their counseling hospitality and wisdom, they should not feel that the lack of specific experience renders them unfit to offer pastoral guidance.

The mental health community is divided on the topic of disclosure. An entire field of peer-to-peer counseling relies on confessing personal lapses and sharing helpful strategies. This philosophy underlies successful group programs such as Alcoholics Anonymous and Weight Watchers. In these settings, the leader functions more as a facilitator who shares personal experiences rather than as a designated authority or teacher, the usual role of the rabbi. In contrast, more traditional schools of psychotherapy suggest that personal questions not be answered directly but that the mental health professional should instead probe these personal questions to understand how they relate to patients' current struggles. It is difficult to emulate this approach in the pastoral context because the congregant already knows a fair amount about the rabbi.

Still, the issue of how to respond to a congregant's question about clergy's past or present private life is not completely straightforward. Simply refusing on principle to answer the congregant's question may feel dismissive and create more distance. Answering the question at face value may, however, deflect from the congregant's problem and derail the intervention. If a high school student asks whether his or her rabbi had ever smoked pot, the rabbi's best answer, regardless of actual past experiences with marijuana is, "I can answer your question directly and we could have a longer conversation about me. But I think it's more helpful to talk about you right now." In most cases, the congregant's curiosity will abate with tactful redirection to the issue at hand. A congregant benefits more from clergy's attentive, religiously informed, compassionate listening than from specific knowledge of the rabbi's past. General advice about what has been helpful to others may be useful, even if the "other" is the rabbi. Sage clergy offer advice from their experience but disguise the source of their wisdom. Two brief stories illustrate this.

Example 24. A familiar story of divorce

In the course of a Talmud study session, a student reveals that his parents are going through an acrimonious separation. The teacher's own parents divorced while she was in college, causing her much personal and academic turmoil. Psychotherapy and swimming helped her come to terms with the distress caused by the turbulent family situation. Without specifying the source of her own wisdom, she responds to the student by drawing from her own saga:

- "This is really tough."
- "I'm happy to speak with you more about your family situation."
- "Talking things out with a psychotherapist can be helpful too. Also, I've known people who find support and strength from non-verbal modalities like exercise and meditation."

Questions to consider

1. When have you shared stories from your past with a congregant?
2. Do you think that the congregant found this experience helpful?

Discussion

Mindful that the student's story resonates with her own, the teacher in the above story formulates an empathic, yet non-directive, response. Her personal experience facilitates her acknowledgment of the pain of a parental rift. It also helps her offer practical strategies for how to cope.

Example 25. The rabbi is asked about his feelings

A couple despairing after a failed attempt at *in vitro* fertilization asks a rabbi who recently became the father of twins through adoption, "Did you and your wife get depressed and argue when you went through infertility?"

Questions to consider

1. Does this request to share personal information feel different from the previous story, Example 24, in which a student reveals that his parents are in the process of divorcing?

Discussion

The rabbi answers empathically but does not linger on his experience: "It was a dark time. Everyone's situation is different, but the fact that we struggled to create our family does give me a firsthand understanding of how tough infertility is on a couple." The rabbi's answer pertains to spiritual struggle and theological inquiry, conversation topics that are prominent in the pastoral relationship. Congregants may ask these kinds of questions because of specific events their lives, such as failure or tragedy. Existential qualms may also emerge from protracted periods of religious alienation. Congregants may question clergy about existential questions because they recognize that clergy, as people who take religious life seriously, are likely to have reckoned with spiritual doubt. Here too, clergy best serve their congregants by validating the common experience of struggles with faith and sharing helpful strategies, rather than detailing the specifics of their own situation. We offer a few pointers to remind you that pastoral counseling is about the congregant and not about you.

*   Do not assume that similar life experience evokes similar feelings.
*   Rather than sharing your specific story, draw from personal experience to offer general wisdom and helpful strategies.

This chapter highlights the importance of clergy's presence and personal life in pastoral counseling. The demands imposed in this area are ongoing and potentially isolating. There are specific means by which clergy can get the support they deserve to maintain their emotional and spiritual health.

Support and supervision

Nothing surpasses the support provided by the collective wisdom of a group of people who trust each other and share similar experiences. Support for clergy should start in seminary and continue throughout vocational life. Clergy look to professional conferences for continuing vocational education and general peer support. However, they have limited opportunities for regular or open discussion of their work. In addition, clergy are reluctant to expose their own struggles and professional challenges. Part of rabbinic reality is pressure to conform in terms of denominational standards and ideology. This may handicap rabbis who might want to discuss or implement more maverick solutions to contemporary problems. Clergy may find comfort in knowing that there is also pressure to conform to industry norms in other vocations, such as academia or politics.

Seminary training generally includes hands-on training, such as hospital chaplaincy or other internships. The value of direct service is directly proportional to the quality of mentorship provided. One-on-one and small-group supervision offer future clergy the opportunity to review rewarding and challenging encounters inherent in the pastoral component of their work. In addition to parsing the issues of specific cases, students become more comfortable sharing their work, asking questions, and revealing vulnerabilities. Upon graduation, rabbis often find themselves feeling isolated in positions where there is a constant demand for guidance and support, yet little replenishment of clergy's precious internal resources. Depletion can lead to dissatisfaction, bitterness, and destructive activity, such as substance abuse or boundary violations. It is imperative that clergy seek and create opportunities for spiritual and psychological support. Alumni gatherings and informal networks help assuage the loneliness inherent in religious work. In addition, rabbis do well to seek out individual supervision with trained personnel and to form peer supervision groups with other local clergy. Mental health professionals regularly present challenging cases to respected colleagues, either for a fee or in a peer consultation arrangement. This same model can work well for clergy, who might contract to meet with a psychologist to review pastoral issues on an individual basis or get together with a peer group of local clergy to discuss difficult cases and share perspectives and resources.

Individual psychotherapy

Along with academic study and spiritual guidance, future clergy deserve the opportunity to explore themselves and their vocations. Individual psychotherapy offers this opportunity. The more students get to know themselves while at seminary, the more they will be available to the full richness of the didactic and experiential components of these formative years. It is important that the administration and faculty of seminaries support psychotherapy by explicitly addressing the stigma often attached to mental health treatment and by offering time and affordable referrals for appointments. Clergy in the field often find it difficult to admit that they need psychological help. However, if they push personal problems under the rug, they run the risk of isolation, burnout, or boundary violations. A positive relationship with psychotherapy during seminary years helps working clergy who experience emotional distress connect to professional mental health support later in their careers if needed.

Spiritual sustenance

The necessity for clergy to make time for personal spiritual development and other scholarly endeavors goes beyond preparing for sermons or answering questions. Text study is critical to nourish the rabbi's spiritual core and replenish the well that maintains a healthy vocation. Some rabbis are in the habit of studying Torah on their own. Others prefer to maintain the tradition of learning in *chevruta*, with a peer. Professional conventions and spiritual retreats are also opportunities to renew inspiration and acquire new skills. Every rabbi also needs a personal *rebbe*, someone to go to for spiritual guidance and mentorship. This may or may not be the same person as a *posek*, who is usually a revered and respected teacher that the rabbi consults for difficult questions of Jewish law or practice.

To be of service, caregivers need to be cared for. This dictum applies to clergy and their families. Rabbis, along with their families, are public figures whose work regularly imposes on their privacy, energy, and time. In order to sustain and replenish themselves, clergy must have confidential settings in which they can let down their guard and discuss matters of faith, vocation, and practice. Peer groups, supervision, and psychotherapy are channels for this kind of support. Clergy also need to make time to maintain their private study of sacred texts. Similarly, rabbis' spouses and children deserve time and attention for the unique challenges they face as clergy families.

Chapter 4

Setting up the pastoral interview

This chapter moves from the conceptual level to more practical issues involved in applying pastoral principles in order to best achieve spiritual and psychological goals. Some of these considerations might seem to reflect a level of detail that may feel trivial at first. However, the cumulative impact of such details is often what enhances or detracts from good pastoral care.

Making the congregant comfortable

The rabbi is a kind of host who should be prepared to receive both regular and unexpected guests. People make visits to clergy for all sorts of reasons. Sometimes the stated reason for the interview doesn't square with the rabbi's assessment, and the congregant spells out just what the congregant needs. At other times, the alleged purpose for a pastoral visit may be a cover for other concerns. Or, as often happens, the congregant initiating the interview does not fully know what motivates the request to meet with the rabbi. The rabbi should always have a counseling hat on and pastoral skills ready. Even routine matters, such as planning a life-cycle celebration, like a *bris* (ritual circumcision) or bat mitzvah, or a community function, such as a charity event or Holocaust commemoration, may generate comments or questions that invite pastoral inquiry. Setting up the interview so as to create an atmosphere of pleasant hospitality prepares clergy and congregants for discussions of the expected and the unexpected.

Our best advice for pastoral hospitality is to let the congregant speak first. The rabbi allows the congregant to speak freely and without interruption for several minutes at the outset of the interview. The congregant's narrative will be very different if allowed to continue without interruption. Important information will be gleaned from what the congregant says without prompting. The rabbi can learn a great deal from paying attention to how the congregant presents a story, how material is organized, and which details are included or left out. All along, the rabbi pays full attention to the congregant's words, emotional tone, and body language, such as eye contact or fidgeting. A skilled interviewer uses facial expressions and brief comments such as "I see" and "Please, tell me more about that" to advance and deepen the interview. The rabbi checks in if something is unclear, "Let me make sure I understand you correctly," and reflects back what the rabbi hears.

Clergy need to keep in mind that the pastoral interview is likely to unfold differently than other conversations. Sometimes it takes the congregant a few moments to get into a difficult topic. The rabbi should not rush to fill the silence. The rabbi who sits still and offers full attention invites the congregant to continue talking. The conversation deepens. While stretches of quiet may feel uncomfortable to the novice interviewer, such moments accrue to create an atmosphere of calm and safety. It is important to be explicit about this technique because in so many other roles, clergy break the ice and speak first. This would be a mistake in pastoral counseling, because setting an agenda or creating expectations can hijack the visit and derail the congregant's intention. The more difficult the material, the more likely it is that the congregant will allow or even encourage clergy to lead the interview.

Where to meet

The physical space in which clergy counsel should create an atmosphere of safety and hospitality. Interviews should be held in dignified, appropriately private settings. The best location for pastoral counseling interviews is an office. When that is not possible, the rabbi may improvise by using a public room, such as a library or classroom.

Some clergy have the practice of meeting congregants in coffee shops or restaurants. While the intent is to put the congregant at ease or to allow the meeting to be interpreted as a social interaction rather than a pastoral visit, meetings in public locations have a high potential to generate curiosity from people passing by and also invite disruption. Meetings in public might also feel safer for the rabbi. Because a rabbi is such a visible leader who has multiple roles, the extent to which the rabbi can conduct a pastoral session in privacy must be tempered by other concerns. The rabbi may worry that there is a greater potential for the congregant to misinterpret the rabbi's intention or even to allege impropriety with a private meeting.

Ideally, the rabbi's office has a curtained window to the outside as well as to the reception area. A pane of glass in the rabbi's office door, for example, is a simple way of satisfying this concern. The congregant can sit with his or her back to the door to maximize privacy. In arranging office furniture, the rabbi should be aware of boundaries and how the space will feel for congregants. One option is for the rabbi to sit behind the desk when meeting with congregants. Alternatively, rabbi and congregant may sit in armchairs facing one another with a small table between the two chairs.

The office should be neat and not overly personal. Although it may seem obvious, this point is being highlighted because the cluttered office of a scholarly professor is a common stereotype that may carry over to clergy. Such an environment does not suit the pastoral counseling situation. The décor of a rabbi's office will differ from that of a mental health professional. A rabbi's study is likely to be lined by many religious books. Unlike the therapist, whose office style aims for maximal neutrality, the rabbi and the rabbi's family are known in the community. Thus, displays of personal life, such as family photos, are not out of place. At the same time, photographs or artwork in the rabbi's office should not bombard the congregant with distractions.

In order to maintain a dignified environment, distractions and interruptions should be minimized as far as possible. It is the rabbi's responsibility to instruct synagogue staff not to interrupt when meetings with congregants are occurring. Clergy should not take phone calls or look at papers, a computer, smartphone, or other devices during a pastoral interview. The congregant will legitimately interpret all such behaviors to mean that the rabbi is more interested in something other than the conversation at hand. If the rabbi is aware of an unfolding congregational crisis or personal situation that might interrupt the interview, the rabbi can inform the congregant of this at the outset, "I want to give you my full attention but I want to let you know that I expect an urgent phone call this morning. If it comes during our meeting, I'll keep it as brief as possible." If the call requires privacy, the rabbi should step outside the office rather than asking the congregant to move.

What about eating or drinking during pastoral interviews? Here again, a combination of the rabbi's personal style coupled with common sense and courtesy offers guidance. Unlike a therapist, who would not share a meal with a patient, a rabbi might invite a congregant to talk over lunch in the rabbi's study. If the rabbi is brewing coffee or tea, the rabbi might offer some to the congregant. Whatever the custom, the clergy office should be clean of debris. In addition to maintaining a neat office, rabbis should monitor their space to make sure that private material is not visible. There is always a natural curiosity about what is on the rabbi's desk. Making sure that documents are concealed not only protects the privacy of the people to whom the material refers but also communicates that the congregant seeking counseling is in a confidential environment.

Though meeting in the rabbi's private study is the ideal location for most pastoral visits, the rabbi will find that it is not always possible to meet congregants in an office or even another public space. Often the rabbi will need to visit the congregant at the congregant's home. When the rabbi needs to make a home visit, the rabbi should try to meet with congregants in public rooms, such as a kitchen or living room, rather than a bedroom. If the congregant is bedridden at home or in the hospital, the rabbi should leave the bedroom door open and sit on a chair at a respectful distance from the bed. Sometimes a counseling session occurs opportunistically, such as when a rabbi and a congregant travel together to a conference, a distant wedding, or simply somewhere local. Such a circumstance might come about by design or arise spontaneously.

Example 26. Counseling in a car

Matthew Green and his wife Simone have been arguing about their son Avi, a high school senior, who announced after winter break that he needs time off after high school and no longer wants to start college in the fall. Matthew thought of discussing the matter with Rabbi Marcus but has not gotten around to it. One Sunday morning in February, Rabbi Marcus mentions that he is going to the airport later in the day. Matthew volunteers to drive the rabbi and asks if they might spend some time discussing a problem he is having with Avi.

Questions to consider

1. Do you feel it is appropriate to discuss sensitive matters while traveling?
2. What do you do when there are several people traveling together and one person starts to talk about a private matter?

Discussion

Rabbi Marcus does not prefer car rides as an optimal location for counseling. At the same time, he realizes that Matthew might be hesitant to disclose a family problem and is more comfortable being in the driver's seat where he is literally in control of the wheel and will not have to sit face to face with the rabbi. The rabbi understands that accepting the car ride is a kind of compromise and is mindful not to give the impression that he barters advice for concrete services. He responds, "If it works for you to drive me to the airport, that's fine, but I want you to know that if this isn't convenient, I'd be happy to meet with you in the office and talk through whatever is going on with you and Avi."

Situations in which clergy are together with individual congregants for extended periods of time, such as when traveling or in waiting rooms, readily turn into impromptu pastoral counseling sessions. While such unplanned encounters may provide just the right opportunity for a person to open up and engage pastoral support, clergy need to keep several factors in mind. These include privacy and confidentiality, as there are likely to be other people within earshot. The rabbi is careful to speak in a low voice and not to mention names. If the rabbi receives a phone call while traveling with others, the rabbi tells the person on the line that other people are around. In addition, the degree to which the rabbi is connected to the congregant makes a difference in an *ad hoc* counseling session. As in the above example, travel with a congregant might yield meaningful pastoral counseling. However, if the person in the adjacent airplane seat is a stranger, the rabbi may or may not want to become involved in a lengthy discussion of personal or spiritual crisis.

Managing time

Pastoral hospitality also requires that clergy frame the length of interviews so that congregants know how much time is available. Many clergy struggle with how to allocate time. It is not always clear how long an interview should be and how many sessions are appropriate and how close together they should be. This includes sessions in the office, home, or hospital visits, as well as time spent on the phone or computer. In the mental health world, time is a precious commodity and is highly regulated and compensated. Sessions are booked and billed for in blocks of 30 or 45 minutes. Therapists are seldom available to patients beyond the predictable session length or outside of conventional hours. Time in the pastoral context rarely conforms to preset expectations.

While clergy do not bill by the hour, their time is as valuable. It is all the more striking that rabbis and their congregants often feel that the rabbi should be available 24/7. While cases of true emergency, such as a life-threatening medical or psychiatric crisis, domestic violence, or death, demand availability in the middle of the night, such situations are few and far between. In a similar vein, rabbis often feel that if they devote enough time and effort to a difficult problem, they will be able to resolve thorny issues. Again, extending the pastoral counseling session rarely results in a neat outcome. Instead, going overtime in a significant way is likely to disrupt the rest of the rabbi's day and negatively affect others whose needs depend on the rabbi being punctual. When a situation is complex, but not urgent, clergy should keep to a reasonable schedule and suggesting a follow-up meeting to continue their pastoral work.

The length of counseling sessions should be defined at the outset. The rabbi is responsible for monitoring time. Thirty to forty-five minutes is a comfortable outer limit for an initial meeting. Congregants fare better with several 20- to 30-minute meetings that allow time to reflect and process than they do with marathon interviews. Attention to time also focuses the interview and defines it as having a serious purpose. The rabbi is responsible for anticipating the end of the session and leaving time to summarize what has been discussed, plan follow-up, and, when needed, make a referral. The rabbi should note that especially long sessions or meetings held at unusual times may lead to unrealistic expectations or misinterpretations. For example, congregants might think that it is okay to contact the rabbi any time, day or night, or that the rabbi has a special interest in the congregant that goes beyond what the rest of the community receives. Additionally, extensive late night conversations, by phone or email, do not conform to professional standards.

Example 27. Not enough time to get to the heart of the matter

Matthew Green is relieved when the Rabbi offers him an opportunity to talk with him about Avi in his office. "Thank you for saying that, Rabbi. It probably would be better for me to come to your office. Would it be okay if Simone comes? She's pretty upset these days."

They set up a time for the next day. At the beginning of the interview, Rabbi Marcus greets Matthew and Simone and frames the session; "We have 20 minutes today to talk about what brought you in to see me. As we get close to the end of the time, we can decide together whether we want to set up another meeting."

Matthew begins, "Rabbi, Avi has always been a good kid. Does his homework, helps out, is nice to his siblings. We always expected that he would go to college after high school. And now, all of a sudden, he tells us he's not going!"

Rabbi Marcus asks the Greens when Avi changed his mind and what was going on. Matthew begins to explain. Simone interjects, "Matthew, you know this isn't the whole story. There's a whole lot that's upsetting Avi. He's worried about leaving the family the way things are at home. You and I both know what the real problem is. I've let this go on for too long, especially with your mother being sick. But now that it's really affecting our kids, it has to stop!"

Matthew and Simone begin to argue. Rabbi Marcus feels pressured. They are past the midpoint of the session. While the Greens' situation is unclear and growing more complex by the moment, the rabbi is responsible for keeping track of time. Five minutes from now, he has a meeting scheduled with a congregant whose father is on life support. He must be on time for that next appointment.

Questions to consider

1. How do you establish how long the interview will be?
2. What do you do when a congregant brings up important material at the last minute?
3. What if your next activity is something less urgent, such as working on your sermon or going for a routine dental appointment? How do you decide when to extend the time or preserve the original frame?

Discussion

Naturally, Rabbi Marcus is concerned that a family he knows and cares about is in trouble. He also wonders what Simone is talking about. However, he must be vigilant about time management. It does not seem as though Matthew and Simone will clarify the picture in the next few minutes. Their situation appears serious but not urgent. Rabbi Marcus does not want to give the impression that, if his curiosity is sufficiently piqued, he will extend the time of the session. He needs to stick to his schedule and the Greens need time to figure out what they are going to reveal to their rabbi. If Rabbi Marcus finds himself motivated to extend the first interview and even encroach on the next congregant's appointment because he feels intrigued or caught up in a sense of drama, it is all the more important for him to reflect on his countertransference.

A few minutes before their designated end time, Rabbi Marcus says, "I do need to stop soon. I don't know what you mean by 'the whole story' or 'the real problem,' but I can tell this is really important. I think you want to talk about this with me, but it's hard. How about we meet again in a few days?"

Rabbi Marcus schedules a second session with the Greens. He begins the next session in a focused way by reminding Matthew and Simone where they left off.

Think about your pastoral counseling practices, and consider how the following suggestions fit in with your current practice.

•   Establish fixed office hours at different times such as during the day, evening, or on Sunday.

- Establish how long the interview will be at the outset and stick to that time.
- Anticipate the end of the interview, give the congregant time to wrap up, and then plan the next step.
- Respond to congregants' communications in a timely fashion.
- Make emergency contact information clear and available.

Example 28. Determining the reason for the visit

After attending a program in the synagogue on family health, Hannah Glaser makes an appointment to see Rabbi Marcus. She is married to Neil, a prominent member of the community, who physically abuses her on a regular basis. Like many abused women, she is reluctant to expose the domestic violence in their home. She worries that either she will not be believed or that her disclosure will get back to Neil and result in a worse situation.

On walking into the rabbi's study, Hannah is not certain how much she will disclose. The rabbi, who does not know about the abuse, notes that Hannah seems tense. He makes a short, neutral opening comment, "Hannah, good to see you. What can I do for you today?" or "Hannah, I understand you have something to talk about today." The rabbi is direct and to the point. This acknowledges the nature of their conversation as a pastoral interview with a specific purpose. He does not encourage Hannah, who is nervous, to go off her intended course.

Hannah starts the visit with a pleasantry, "Hello Rabbi, how are you and the family? I heard that your mother was in town."

Questions to consider

1. How do you balance "breaking the ice" with "cutting to the chase"?
2. What strategies do you use to encourage the congregant to reveal a problem?

Discussion

Rabbi Marcus knows that sometimes congregants use idle conversation as a way to avoid getting to the point. Thus, he answers questions about himself and his family in a very abbreviated manner and redirects the conversation back to the congregant. "Hannah, thanks for asking how my family is doing. I appreciate it, and I want to make sure we also have time to discuss what's on your mind. What brings you in today?" Rabbi Marcus's careful listening clues him in to the possibility that his congregant's hesitancy has meaning. Hannah may choose to confide her problem or she may retreat and close down the conversation. Either way, the rabbi's patient attention communicates his ongoing availability to listen and explore at her pace.

Take a moment to reflect on your own listening style. When do you feel engaged, distracted, or disinterested? Here are some guidelines to frame your listening:

- Let the congregant take the lead as you listen closely.
- Pay attention to tone and body language, as well as words.
- Mirror what you have heard. Check in and confirm that you understand what the congregant wants you to know.

While most pastoral situations are not urgent and can unfold over time, the rabbi must also be attuned to signs of acute distress or emergency. If Hannah divulges any hints of danger, Rabbi Marcus must be prepared to explore this further and take appropriate steps.

Listening to your emotional pulse

This section focuses on using one's own feelings in pastoral counseling. A fundamental axiom is evaluating urgency. This means that clergy need to determine when a congregant is in imminent danger. This includes the threat of self-harm, harm to others, or harm by others. While such situations are rare, clergy must be prepared to access emergency services.

To return to Rabbi Marcus's interview with Hannah, as soon as Rabbi Marcus inquires about why Hannah has come to see him, Hannah begins to cry. She reveals that Neil has hit her on many occasions. This comes as a shock to Rabbi Marcus. He struggles to get a grip on his reaction. He says, "Tell me more about this." Rabbi Marcus listens carefully and asks questions that will call for specific behavioral examples, so that he can determine if Hannah is in acute danger. For example, he asks her to describe how Neil hits her and about the events that precede the hitting, as well as what happens after. He asks whether Hannah has needed medical treatment for any injuries caused by Neil, if the children have been involved, and if anyone has ever noticed or questioned any injuries. The rabbi asks these questions because they help establish whether Hannah is in danger. The rabbi asks about other behaviors associated with domestic violence, such as whether Neil has restricted Hannah's social life or access to money. Rabbi Marcus makes sure to ask Hannah if she feels safe at the present time. Depending on what he learns, Rabbi Marcus helps Hannah formulate a plan responsive to her situation and level of perceived danger. He is prepared with a list of referrals that include the address of a safe house for victims of domestic violence and the names of therapists and lawyers experienced in this area. He asks Hannah what she wants to do and whether she feels she can return home.

The rabbi asks these questions not because the details are interesting but because inadequate detail may lead to an inflated or insufficient response. Rabbi Marcus checks in with his outrage at hearing Hannah's accusation. He identifies disbelief as well as the wish to protect her. This is because Rabbi Marcus knows Neil, and the rabbi has trouble believing that Neil is that kind of person. Rabbi Marcus wonders briefly whether Hannah is trying to get attention and whether she is exaggerating her home situation or even lying. The more concrete details that Hannah provides, the more the rabbi can appropriately contextualize his feelings about her and Neil. If Rabbi Marcus becomes increasingly concerned about Hannah's safety and she is reluctant to take action such as contacting a lawyer or going to a safe house, he will have to deal with his distress as well as her passivity. Many people in abusive relationships are scared to upset the status quo, however bad it may be. The rabbi's job in such a situation is to strengthen his alliance with Hannah, buy time, and build her confidence to partner with him and other appropriate consultants. What the rabbi should not do is bypass Hannah and make interventions such as calling Neil directly. Such action puts her in greater danger.

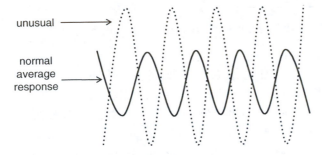

Figure 4.1 Taking your emotional pulse.

If the rabbi feels that Neil has abused the children, he needs to get the advice of local child protection services to determine his role as a mandated reporter.

The rabbi's own feelings while listening serve as a kind of professional barometer that informs practical pastoral interventions. Identifying strong feelings that depart from the rabbi's baseline is a critical skill in pastoral counseling. Any significant shift in the rabbi's state of mind or heart should be seen as a signal to pause and reflect on what has been stirred up in the rabbi's own psychology. From the time of anticipating a first meeting with a congregant and continuing on throughout the interview, the rabbi checks in with his or her feelings. All clergy have an index of personal responses. Self-awareness is the most valuable instrument in gauging when a response deviates from the rabbi's usual evenly hovering baseline of paying attention. An image of overlapping sine waves gives visual representation of this idea. The solid line in Figure 4.1 indicates a conventional response; the dotted wave denotes reactions that alert the rabbi to pay extra attention.

During the interview, the rabbi checks in for feelings of anxiety, boredom, and excitement. Does the rabbi find the congregant credible, manipulative, alluring, annoying, or repellant? The mantra of checking one's emotional pulse bears repeating. Each rabbi needs to be aware of hot buttons. In other words, the rabbi stays alert to the personality types, interactions, and topics that provoke strong feelings. The next three stories illustrate clergy responses to feelings of concern, anger, and surprise.

Example 29. The rabbi worries about a congregant

Rabbi Jack Stein notices that Aliza Golding, a student who attended Hillel events with enthusiasm earlier in the semester, has been absent for several weeks. He emails Aliza and invites her to have coffee, a common practice for him with students. As Rabbi Jack spots Aliza approaching the campus café, he notices that she looks much thinner. Concerns about a medical illness, depression, or eating problems cross his mind. As the conversation progresses, Aliza discloses that her five-year old brother has been diagnosed with autism and her mother is not coping well with this news. Aliza tries to go home most weekends to help out. She is struggling to keep up with her course work. The eating disorder, which she battled in high school, has returned.

Questions to consider

1. What feelings are stirred in you by Aliza's story?
2. How would you intervene to help this student?

Discussion

As he listens to Aliza, Rabbi Jack feels sad and upset. He detects rescue wishes in himself. Rabbi Jack is aware that the strength of these feelings exceeds his usual response to students in distress. Aliza reminds Rabbi Jack of a girl he knew in high school who wrote him sad poetry and was later hospitalized for a sleeping-pill overdose. Jack Stein is also worried about his wife Miriam and their new baby, who has a heart problem. As his coffee date with Aliza progresses, Rabbi Jack checks his emotional pulse and realizes that the worry and protective tenderness he feels towards her are different from his usual level of concern for students. He recognizes that while Aliza faces significant challenges, his heightened countertransference comes from other sources. Memories of his high school classmate as well as the current strain in his family are having an impact on his perception and judgment.

The goal of Rabbi Jack's meeting with Aliza is to touch base with her and remind her that he and the Hillel community are there for support. His role is to remain available. What he should not do is insert himself directly into the situation. Feelings that go above and beyond the need to stay in touch alert Rabbi Jack to pay extra attention to his behavior with Aliza in the here and now. Thus, he is mindful of his tone in speaking with her. He is careful not to respond to her emails outside of conventional hours. While she certainly needs support during this difficult time, she needs a caring rabbi, not a romantic hero.

Example 30. The rabbi is offered a bribe

Aaron Davis, a synagogue board member estranged from his wife, meets with Rabbi Kane. He tries to enlist the rabbi as an advocate in his bitter divorce negotiation. Aaron suggests that if Rabbi Kane is successful in brokering the custody battle, Aaron will ensure that her contract is renewed with a generous salary increase.

Questions to consider

1. How do you respond to veiled bribes or threats?
2. Can you salvage a pastoral relationship after you feel insulted or threatened?

Discussion

When Rabbi Kane hears Aaron proffer financial reward in exchange for biased rabbinic support, she feels an anger that exceeds her usual exasperation with inappropriate congregant demands. Her awareness helps her maintain extra vigilance and suppress her impulse to launch into an angry diatribe in response to Aaron's unethical suggestion. Rabbi Kane understands that Aaron is used to getting his way and is humiliated by his failed marriage. Rather than dismiss her congregant as an entitled bully, Rabbi Kane explains to Aaron that she feels her rabbinic role mandates that she help the entire Davis family negotiate the painful transition of divorce. Rabbi Kane adds that she hopes that Aaron will continue his involvement with the synagogue because she values his importance to the community. While the rabbi has to make clear that there cannot be any quid pro quo, she tries to do so in a way that does not alienate Aaron from seeking her help or participating in Jewish life.

Example 31. The rabbi meets with an ambivalent mourner

One morning after *minyan* (morning prayer services), Rabbi Daniel Marcus learns that Bennet Ruskin, the father of a congregant, Joe, died the previous evening in a nearby suburb. Rabbi Marcus calls Joe immediately, apologizes for not having known that his dad was ill, and asks if he might come over to visit and help Joe prepare for the funeral. Rabbi Marcus notes that Joe is unusually terse on the phone. He assumes this is due to shock and grief.

Rabbi Marcus finds Joe sitting alone in his kitchen. As he begins to offer his condolences in person, Joe interrupts the rabbi, "Don't bother, rabbi. My father was a bad person, a delinquent husband and father. He cheated on my mother and pilfered money from my bar mitzvah account. It would be tough enough just going to the funeral, but on top of it, my mother has asked me to speak on behalf of the children. I know that Jewish tradition holds that children have an obligation to honor their parents, but I don't respect my father and I feel like my mother was pathetic for staying with him. For sure I can't imagine knocking myself out to say *kaddish* for him for a whole eleven months."

Questions to consider

1. How would you deal with your surprise at hearing the congregant's negative feelings about his father?
2. How would you advise a designated mourner who has ambivalent or hostile feelings about the deceased?

Discussion

The death of a parent is a watershed moment in life. Throughout the trajectory of acute loss and bereavement, the rabbi is a key person who offers comfort, religious guidance, and support. Most of the time, this work is in the nature of consolation. However, the rabbi must also be prepared for both subtle and, as in this case, overt expressions of ambivalence or frank negativity towards the deceased.

While Rabbi Marcus may be startled or even shocked by Joe's remarks, he knows that death can provoke a cascade of raw feeling. The rabbi understands that neither critique nor refutation of Joe's disquieting accusations and expressions of contempt will help. Instead, he listens to him with compassion. Rabbi Marcus's job is not to establish the true nature of Bennet Ruskin's life or role as a husband and father. Rather, the rabbi best serves his congregant by helping Joe navigate the immediate hurdles imposed by his father's death. Rabbi Marcus's deeper goal is to communicate that Jewish tradition can help Joe metabolize painful feelings while he receives the support of the community.

Rabbi Marcus quickly establishes his priorities. First, Joe needs practical advice regarding the eulogy. Next, he needs strategies on how to get through *shiva*, where there is likely to be an outpouring of sympathy. Rabbi Marcus's job is to help Joe manage his feelings while facilitating a dignified funeral for his father. Rabbi Marcus knows that it will not serve Joe well if he makes a spectacle of himself by losing control in a public setting. He draws upon his alliance with Joe as he offers guidance.

Rabbi: I hear that you have hard feelings about your father. I don't doubt what you say about him. But this isn't the time to bring them out. I suggest that you opt out of giving the eulogy. There is no Jewish obligation for a specific person, such as a child, to eulogize the dead.[1]

Joe: But my mother wants me to. Neither my sister nor brother will do it.

Rabbi: None of you has to. A neutral person like a rabbi, like me, can speak. A funeral is not the correct forum to bring up these kinds of feelings. You do need to express them, but privately. I'm here for you to talk about this more, over time. It's important that the funeral be dignified.

Joe: Okay. I can see getting through the funeral if someone else gives the eulogy. But what about the *shiva*? I can't deal with all these people coming over and telling me what a great guy my dad was.

Rabbi: There are a lot of ways to handle that. When your friends come to visit you, you don't have to lie. You can be judicious.

Joe: What about if people come and say things that just ring so false to me?

Rabbi: You don't have to agree with them. You can just say "Thank you." If it gets too hard, you can limit the hours of *shiva* and make it private.[2]

Joe: Couldn't I just skip *shiva* altogether?

Rabbi: I don't suggest that. I've been a rabbi for a long time and I appreciate the power of *shiva*. It's important to have this time to devote to loss. In many ways you have had to deal with feelings of loss for a long time because betrayal is a form of loss, and your father did betray you. *Shiva* is exactly the appropriate time for you to mourn the relationship you wish you might have had with your father, but didn't. You may not want to give the eulogy, but you are a mourner, and you need to go through this mourning process. *Shiva* is designed for people to cope with the unfinished business that happens when a parent dies.

Joe: What about *kaddish*? What will people think of me if I don't do it?

Rabbi: Your father might have wanted someone to say *kaddish* for him. If you can't commit to it, I can arrange for someone to say it for him on a daily basis. Let's try to say it together at the funeral and at the *shiva*. After that, we'll take it one day at a time.

Joe: Okay, Rabbi, one day at a time.

The above scenarios describe situations that are within the realm of clergy encounters. Life circumstances offer clergy multiple opportunities to enter congregants' lives at emotionally charged moments. In order to be effective, clergy need to pay attention to their own emotional pulses.

- Pay attention to what you are feeling.
- Your gut response is an important guide to danger, crisis, and complexity.

Taking notes

Keeping track of information supports and dignifies pastoral counseling. Situations that feel vivid in the moment often fade in memory, leaving well-intentioned clergy struggling to recall important data. It is a good practice for the rabbi to keep records of pastoral involvement. This includes making notes of face-to-face conversations and phone calls, as well as filing text messages and emails. A rabbi, educator, or other spiritual leader might keep a pad handy during a live interview and offer the simple explanation, "You have come to me with an important matter. I find it helpful to make notes so that I keep track of information." If an important conversation occurs in a setting where taking notes is inappropriate, such as at a social gathering, in a dire medical situation, or while engaging in another activity, such as travel or sports, the rabbi should make it a priority to jot down notes as soon as possible.

Clergy templates for notes should include:

- name(s) of congregant(s)
- date of contact (phone call, interview, etc.)
- preparation – how the matter came to the rabbi's attention, why the meeting was scheduled
- pertinent family information (this is especially helpful when discussing life-cycle events such as b'nei mitzvah celebrations, weddings, and funerals)
- a summary of what happened during the meeting
- plan for follow-up (this includes putting a reminder in the rabbi's calendar to check in if appropriate).

Payment for pastoral counseling

Clergy do not charge for pastoral counseling with their congregants. Rabbis do not bill for counseling sessions held in their offices, hospital visits, or for phone conversations. The absence of clear compensation for these important functions might be attractive to some congregants who are reluctant to either admit the need for counseling or pay for such services from a mental health provider. At the same time, rabbis need to earn a living and manage their time. Clergy contracts should specify what responsibilities are covered by salary. While the contract may not quantify how much time is to be allocated for pastoral work, there will be a general expectation for counseling. Rabbis need to monitor the extent of their involvement and pay attention to when counseling commitments infringe on other duties. For example, if a rabbi starts to feel that extra compensation should be forthcoming for a particular case, this alerts the rabbi to an important countertransference and signals that it may be time for extra help. This might include discussing the case with a colleague or supervisor. The rabbi needs to clarify just what is taking up extra time or emotional effort and whether referring the congregant to a professional with expertise in the area of need is in order. If the rabbi finds that a certain kind of pastoral counseling is in high demand, such as issues related to the lives of older members, the rabbi might try and bring in auxiliary services, such as a part-time social worker.

Many rabbis do accept payment for clergy functions that require extra time, such as performing weddings and funerals. Others prefer that donations be made to charity or a discretionary fund. Gifts also express appropriate gratitude or recognition. A chaplain may graciously accept a book from a family that she visited many times during their child's hospital stay or a rabbi may accept a clock from the congregation on the occasion of completing an advanced degree. Gifts that are excessive should be declined in a tactful manner. Clergy should also ensure that congregants do not perceive a differential gradient of attention based on wealth. If the aforementioned family offers the same chaplain a large gift certificate or expensive watch, the chaplain courteously suggests that they donate the value of that gift to a charity related to their child's recovery, such as the pediatric playroom or a fund to help out-of-town families. Here are some basic guidelines regarding gifts:

• Establish appropriate fees for non-pastoral clergy functions.
• Discuss the issue of payment before providing a pastoral service.
• Only accept material gifts that are of appropriate value.
• Give thought to intangible "freebies," such as staying in a congregant's vacation home.

Notes

1 In addition to the requirement for a child to mourn his or her parents (see Shulchan Aruch Yoreh Deah 374:4, 380–395 for specifics), all those who will inherit money from the deceased are required to contribute from the estate to the costs of a proper eulogy and burial (see Shulchan Aruch Yoreh Deah 348:2). There is no obligation to

personally give the eulogy. For an extensive discussion on the question of mourning for abusive parents, see Wolowelsky 2010.

2 One may not visit mourners if they have indicated that they do not want visitors at that time (See Shulchan Aruch Yoreh Deah 376:1). Presumably, this applies even if they do not want visitors for the entire week.

Reference

Wolowelsky, Joel (2010). "Mourning Abusive Parents," *Hakirah* 9 (Winter): 191–198.

Chapter 5

Understanding what you hear

The pastoral interview is designed to create an atmosphere of respect in which the congregant feels safe to disclose important and sensitive information. Clergy gather information throughout the interview via active listening and thoughtful questioning. As the congregant discloses, the rabbi needs to analyze the content of what is being said and make sense of it in order to rank priorities, establish goals, and pick a course of action.

The first few minutes of an interview are like learning a code. While the congregant is talking, It is important that the rabbi does not think about what to say next. Rather, the rabbi concentrates on listening and begins to understand the congregant's needs. The first few minutes also offer a counterpart experience for the congregant to read the rabbi's pastoral code. The congregant, who is likely to feel nervous about explaining a problem, unconsciously tunes in to cues such as posture, eye contact, and quality of speech that signal the rabbi's level of engagement. Whether the interview deepens or, conversely, stalls depends on this choreography. The rabbi's understanding of the layers of the congregant's problem will evolve and change as more information accumulates. The rabbi can offer help, which may include religious guidance, practical advice, further consultation, or, in cases of crisis, emergency intervention. A set of basic questions that the rabbi keeps in mind as a framework while conducting the interview helps organize material and establish priorities.

- What is the congregant's most pressing need right now?
- What issues await further exploration?
- What is the rabbi's order of priorities?

In Example 27, Rabbi Marcus communicates concern and even-handed commitment to both Matthew and Simone. By the end of the interview, he realizes that Avi's decision to back out of college has multiple determinants, the most serious of which the rabbi does not yet know. While the matter is somewhat time-sensitive in terms of Avi's plans for the coming year, the rabbi does not detect imminent crisis or danger. Rabbi Marcus notes that his attention is drawn to the unexpected topic, "the real problem" that Simone brought up late in the conversation. He wonders what she means. Still, by the end of the interview, Rabbi Marcus does not feel a sense of urgency when Simone alludes to something that "has been going on for too long ... and now has to stop." He notes that while Simone is upset, she seems to be in control. If Rabbi Marcus felt alarm, this might signal a need for crisis intervention. He might, for example, ask a directed question a few minutes before the end of the interview such as "Is there something else that we haven't gotten to yet that is urgent for you to tell me today?" The situation is very different in Example 28, in which Rabbi Marcus discovers that Hannah Glaser faces clear and present danger that demands immediate attention.

Formulating a hypothesis

As the pastoral interview progresses, the rabbi creates a mental list that ranks the issues according to importance. The rabbi formulates a hypothesis that organizes the material presented and establishes a list of goals. The rabbi asks questions and checks in with the congregant to make sure that the congregant feels understood. The rabbi is not embarrassed to pause when feeling confused or uncertain as to what is going on: "I want to make sure I understand you correctly, did you mean ..." or, "I wasn't clear on what you just said, could you please explain that again?" While forming impressions, the rabbi stays open to new information and ideas. This process of gathering fresh material and gleaning new insights guides ongoing revision of the initial hypothesis. Over time, clergy become more practiced at tuning in to cues that hint at issues beneath the surface of the stated reason for the meeting. Sometimes the congregant puts the problem right out in the open. At other times, the stated reason does not feel like the whole story and needs more unpacking. Some degree of imagination helps clergy generate hypotheses that in turn guide subsequent listening, choice of questions, and interventions.

As an example, during his meeting with the Greens, Rabbi Marcus revises his hypothesis several times. First, he understands that Matthew is anxious about his son. Matthew's request that he bring Simone to the counseling session suggests that the Greens share concern for their son. When Simone enters the conversation, her cryptic words shake up the interview. She seems to subsume Avi's issue under a much more pressing, not yet named problem. By the end of the session, Rabbi Marcus's focus of concern shifts from Avi to the Greens' marriage. He wonders whether Matthew is in the throes of complicated bereavement for his late mother, dire financial straits, a health situation of his own, an affair, or is abusing alcohol or drugs. Consider how you feel reading this case:

How did you understand the story by the end of the interview?
Did your hypothesis change from the beginning of the interview?

This case illustrates how careful listening elicits a flow of pastoral objectives. The next step is to organize and rank these goals.

Setting up a hierarchy of goals

Clergy establish a hierarchy of goals to prioritize which situations are emergencies and must be dealt with immediately and which can wait until a subsequent interview. Typically, issues that come to pastoral attention are multidimensional. It is overwhelming and inefficient to try and address them all at once. A better method is to break down presenting problems into component parts and then approach each problem one at a time. In addition to de-escalating anxiety for the congregant(s), and often the rabbi as well, this technique helps determine how to deploy resources. Part of creating a hypothesis and establishing a hierarchy of goals is planning ahead. Throughout each of these stages, the rabbi considers how to take future steps, such as involving additional family members, recruiting other consultants or community resources, and planning follow-up.

Example 32. The rabbi learns something new

By the end of Example 27, Rabbi Marcus's goal became identifying what Simone calls "the real problem." Whether the explanation is along the lines of his hypotheses, or something else
entirely, Rabbi Marcus is prepared to hear information that may
be painful or humiliating. He assumes that the situation is not
likely to be resolved that day, and so, before the end of the meeting, he suggests that he and the Greens meet again in the near
future. The rabbi also anticipates that before walking out the
door, Matthew and Simone will need to regroup from the swirl of
issues and feelings generated.

Rabbi Marcus interrupts Simone and Matthew's argument
with a comment intended to bring the unspoken to light, "I'm
getting the picture that this is something we will not be able to set-
tle quickly. We only have five more minutes left today. Something
serious is going on in your family, and I don't know yet what that
is. I suggest that we make another appointment. Let's hold off on
talking about Avi's plan for next year and use the rest of this time
to talk about what's going on with the two of you."

Simone blurts out, "It's his drinking, Rabbi! Haven't you seen
how much scotch Matthew knocks back at kiddush? And that's
not all. He's been getting drunk on weeknights as well."

Questions to consider

1. Under what conditions do you extend interviews?
2. How have your hypotheses about the Greens shifted?
3. Do you alter your goals?

Discussion

Rabbi Marcus is indeed surprised but tries not to show it. While he
notices that Matthew enjoys kiddush, he has not registered that his
congregant drinks too much. The rabbi knows that he can assess
Matthew's alcohol use by asking specific questions about the frequency

and quantity of his drinking and the consequences. However, Rabbi Marcus does not have time to do this because the end of the session is near. "This is important information. We need to end soon. I want to give you both a few moments to think about what has come up today and what we need to talk about next. Let's sum up together and plan to meet in a few more days."

Readers may find the analogy of deep-sea diving helpful here. Divers need to pace their ascent from the ocean's depths in order to avoid getting the bends. Similarly, at the end of a heated pastoral counseling meeting, congregants need to readjust their emotional equilibrium. It is clergy's job to bring an interview to a dignified close. The congregant who leaves the interview feeling composed is more likely to heed the rabbi's advice. Further, the congregant will be more disposed to return and seek consultation in the future if the rabbi has created an atmosphere of emotional stability. In this vignette, the sudden introduction of new material causes Rabbi Marcus to revise his hypothesis. His initial understanding of the problem was that Avi was reluctant to go to college. The rabbi planned to ask more about Avi. Now, the focus has shifted to Matthew's alcohol use and its impact on his marriage and family. Rabbi Marcus's goal in the last five minutes of the interview is to sum up what he has learned thus far and then set up a second interview to explore matters further.

Example 33. An extramarital crisis

Jordan and Mira Stone, ages 34 and 33, have been married for nine years and are the parents of three young children. They belong to Rabbi Daniel Marcus's synagogue and live a few houses down the street from the rabbi and his family. One day, Mira calls Rabbi Marcus from the airport crying hysterically as she waits for her flight home from a work conference. She reports that two nights earlier she was having drinks with a colleague from another city and woke up in his bed the next morning. She says that she doesn't remember everything that happened. Mira admits that while the two of them had indulged in email flirtation, she didn't think it would lead to actual sexual activity, but everything happened so fast. She asks the rabbi if she has to tell her husband.

Rabbi Marcus advises Mira to hold off making any confessions until after he and Mira meet in person. However, by the time the rabbi reconnects with her 24 hours later, she has blurted out the story to Jordan, who says he doesn't believe it.

Questions to consider

1. How do you establish a hierarchy of goals in this situation?
2. When do you feel that confession of wrongdoing is helpful, and when do you determine that it is harmful?

Discussion

At the time of hearing Mira's agitated confession, Rabbi Marcus identifies three immediate goals. First, he has to advise her as to the status of her relationship with her husband from the perspective of Jewish law, which weighs a wife's infidelity differently than that of a husband.[1] Second, he notes that if there has not already been marital discord, there certainly will be now. Third, he is concerned about the potential medical consequences to Mira as a result of sexual activity with her colleague. Rabbi Marcus's instinct to slow things down until he could talk with Mira face to face was correct. Mira's disregard for this suggestion and her sense of urgency to confess are points that the rabbi keeps in mind and comes back to at a later time.

From the Jewish legal stance, the details of what actually occurred between Mira and her colleague are foggy. The facts that she was under the influence of alcohol and that there were no witnesses give the rabbi a lot of latitude to keep the marriage intact.[2] On the other hand, such events do not happen in a vacuum. Extensive flirting with a colleague on email is a sign that a spouse is engaging in a fantasy that distracts him or her from confronting boredom, anger, or whatever else is off-kilter in the marriage, rather than working on marital problems. Mira will have to come to understand that her actions began well before the actual sexual encounter. Rabbi Marcus thinks of two contradictory hypotheses. One is that Mira's quick disclosure to Jordan indicates that she wants to rein in the situation before she does further damage. Whether or not she had full sexual relations with her colleague, she is sufficiently afraid of the potential consequences of her flirtation. The rabbi's alternate hypothesis is that Mira's confession suggests that she harbors an unconscious wish to sabotage her marriage. Rabbi Marcus realizes that his immediate role is not to unravel Mira's motivation, although that work will need to be done at some point. His immediate goal is to protect her and her family from impulsive disintegration. He might suggest that just to be sure from a medical point of view, Mira undergo a process similar to rape victims, including determination of STD exposure or pregnancy. Of course, a positive pregnancy test does not necessarily confirm that Mira had sex with her colleague, but the rabbi does not neglect these medical considerations. By advising Mira in this way, Rabbi Marcus also signals that he is able to deal with anything that might have occurred.

Rabbi Marcus understands that Jordan's denial may represent his fear that Jewish law will not permit the marriage to continue. The rabbi has an important role in explaining that the facts do not suggest that the marriage must be dissolved from a Jewish legal perspective but that the couple's situation demands attention. That is, once the rabbi has reassured the couple that they can remain married, he is in a key position to assist them in getting to work on their troubled relationship. Rabbi Marcus's biggest contribution to a positive outcome is to slow down the sense of urgency and action. In such situations, emotions run high and a week or two may allow a more nuanced perspective to emerge. The rabbi accepts Jordan and Mira as a legitimately married couple and directs them to focus on their marital issues. These might include feeling taken for granted, sexual problems, different expectations regarding religious practice, involvement with extended family, financial struggles, and so on. This work will best be accomplished over a period of time with a couples' counselor and not the rabbi. Rabbi Marcus needs to stay present as a religious guide for Mira and Jordan as individuals, as a couple, and for their family. For the rabbi to engage in deep exploration of the intimate landscape of their marriage is likely to make Jordan, Mira, and even the rabbi uncomfortable and avoidant. Effective couples work necessitates the exposure of private information and strong feelings that are likely to interfere with the clergy–congregant relationship. Rabbi Marcus schedules a follow-up visit with the couple in his office in several weeks or months to check how they are progressing with their marital issues.

As noted earlier, Jewish law ascribes different significance and consequences to extramarital relations on the part of wives as compared to that of husbands. However, if the situation had been reversed, and Jordan had called from the airport, Rabbi Marcus's pastoral response would have been the same. That is, the rabbi would have placed his major concern on the fact that this marriage is in trouble. While infidelity is common, the reasons behind it need to be understood and addressed. For a couple to get beyond the affair requires commitment to joint exploration and honesty.

Summing up and making a plan

The pastoral intervention is based on a short-term model of one to two sessions, with a limit of five. As soon as the congregant discloses a problem, the rabbi should start to develop a plan. This means that as the rabbi listens, checks his or her own emotional pulse, assesses urgency, asks questions, gathers information, shapes a hypothesis, and ranks priorities, the rabbi also thinks about what will happen after the session ends and how many more sessions will be helpful. As the time for the initial interview comes to a close, the rabbi shares impressions with the congregant. They decide together how to move forward.

A single meeting may provide the clarification, support, and advice that the congregant needs. For example:

- Parents come to Dr. Ellen Shapiro to discuss summer programs for their 12-year-old son. The mother wants the child to further his basketball talent, while the father's emphasis is on an immersive Jewish experience. When Dr. Shapiro suggests a camp that offers both, the parents agree that this is a good compromise.
- An observant congregant consults Rabbi Marcus about attending a nephew's church wedding to a non-Jewish woman. The rabbi discusses several options for the congregant's consideration.

The closing phase of a pastoral interview is especially significant in cases where the situation that led to the initial visit with the rabbi has not been resolved. If both the rabbi and congregant feel that another meeting would be helpful, they schedule a second session. Other family members or relevant persons might be asked to join the next meeting.

If the rabbi feels that the services of another professional, such as a physician, mental health professional, or lawyer are needed, the rabbi guides the congregant on how to access that expertise.

Whether pastoral counseling helps congregants negotiate a rite of passage, sustain heartbreak, rebuild after loss, work through difficult life events, or change behavior, the rabbi's goal is to move people from their current baseline towards greater religious awareness, healthier choices, and fuller connection with Jewish tradition. In some cases, clergy will encounter intractable congregants or face challenges that defy intervention. It is hard to maintain empathy for people whose deeply ingrained patterns show little movement, however much their dysfunction limits their lives or causes misery in the lives of others. Such everyday examples include the tyrannized spouse who stays in an abusive marriage, an alcoholic who continues to drink, or a talented person who sabotages his or her own success. At the same time that clergy struggle to understand why people cling to seemingly suboptimal attitudes or behaviors, they also pay attention to their own expectations. If not acknowledged and dealt with, feelings of failed transformation or more subtle disappointments will cause rabbis to become apathetic or bitter over time. Even when desired outcomes with congregants are not achieved, clergy must find gratification over the long haul of their vocational life. They should not feel that they must continue counseling until the problem is solved. Three examples demonstrate pastoral encounters with different agendas and conclusions.

Example 34. Visiting the parent of a sick child

Rabbi Shira Kane makes a visit to the hospital room of David Draper, a 14-month-old admitted for acute leukemia. The boy is sleeping and his father, Lenny, is sitting in a chair next to him.

Rabbi: Hello. I'm Rabbi Kane, the Jewish chaplain. I came by to visit.
Lenny: Oh.
Rabbi: How are you doing?
[Lenny motions over to David in his crib.]
Rabbi: It's very difficult to see your child suffer.

Lenny: I've had a lot of suffering in my life. I lost my mother to colon cancer when I was 17. There's been a lot of cancer in my family.

Rabbi: So how do you cope with what's going on with this little one here?

Lenny: I'm not scared. Whatever will be will be. I just need to be strong. I need to be there for him. And I'm a strong guy.

Rabbi: I can see that.

Lenny: Look, life gives us all kinds of suffering, and it's our choice how to respond. I was raised religious, and I respect the lifestyle. But the truth is that religion was given to human beings to make us feel better. And the truth is way beyond religion. Sorry if I'm offending you.

Rabbi: Don't worry, you're not. But let me ask you, do you ever feel like you need an outlet for all of this?

Lenny: An outlet? I just don't let it in. When I took this little guy to the doctor, and he gave us the diagnosis of leukemia, my first reaction was "So what do we have to do?" No tears, no emotion, just action. And the doctor looked at me and said "How strong is this guy!" I'm very strong.

Rabbi: Sounds like you've been through a great deal.

Lenny: Look, the most important thing for me is my relationship with my kids. My father was a very tough guy. He worked hard, but there wasn't much money, and he didn't have much time. I am the oldest. Once my mother died, I had to help take care of the little kids.

Rabbi: How sad. It must have been really tough for you.

Lenny: My grandma tried to help, but she was a mess herself.

Rabbi: It sounds like your early life was hard.

Lenny: It was very hard. My parents let me down. But in the end, it is a blessing. Because of my father's lousy relationship with me, my kids and I have the most completely open relationships.

Rabbi: What a story. So much suffering, but you show so much courage.

Lenny: Yes, it's a lot. But I really feel blessed.

Rabbi: Would you like to say a prayer with me for David?

Lenny: Okay, if you think it works. His name is David Zecharia ben Baila. I think prayers are just there to comfort people. My wife likes to know that people pray for David. But thank you for listening. Even if you can never really understand what I feel. Not even my wife can. I guess it's God's design that none of us can truly understand one another.

Rabbi: It's been good talking with you. I look forward to meeting your wife. I'll stop by tomorrow.

Questions to consider

1. What are the challenges of initiating a "cold call" visit as compared to when a congregant requests a pastoral visit?
2. How much would you probe the father's story or challenge his defenses?
3. What would your goal be, and how would you end the visit?

Discussion

Clergy in general, and chaplains in particular, often initiate contact. This contrasts with a mental health encounter, where the patient typically requests a meeting. Entering a scene to which one has not been invited puts the weight of generating momentum on clergy. Some people brusquely dismiss a hospital chaplain whereas others are eager to talk. Over time, Rabbi Kane has evolved her own protocol. Her first goal is to introduce herself to patients and families so that they identify her as a Jewish resource person during their stay in the hospital. She knows that her visits may reveal problems for which there are no solutions. She encourages congregants to express feelings while at the same time supporting their inherent strengths. Parents of sick children respond to clergy in many different ways. Lenny responds to the rabbi's query about his welfare with a wordless motion. Rabbi Kane, who has initiated the visit, sits quietly for a few minutes to give Lenny time to speak. When he remains silent, she offers a general comment designed to express empathy and encourage him to talk, "It's very difficult to see your child suffer." These words catalyze a flow of words that reveal much information about this distressed father's personal history. Rabbi Kane's comment also gives Lenny permission to express negative feelings in her presence should he want to.

Rabbi Kane notes Lenny's repeated use of the word "strong" in describing himself. She understands that he has suffered many traumas and needs to shore up his defenses. Rabbi Kane deliberately chooses not to pick up and explore Lenny's past history of losses. This is in direct contrast to what a mental health professional would do in an ongoing therapy situation. As a chaplain, Rabbi Kane recognizes that while Lenny's dramatic style likely conceals significant vulnerability, it would not be helpful for her to point out his defensive style that is protecting him from feeling weak and helpless. Instead, Rabbi Kane directs her efforts in support of his resilience. Similarly, she is nonplussed when Lenny apologizes for his perceived lapse of belief. Her role as chaplain is not to critique or correct congregants' religious skepticism but rather to show them that Jewish tradition is responsive to suffering and doubt. In this spirit, she asks if she might say a prayer on behalf of the sick baby. Rabbi Kane interprets Lenny's recitation of his son's Hebrew name as indicating his acceptance of her support. She says the prayer and concludes the visit by announcing her plan to visit the next day.

Example 35. A story with two possible endings

Alex, an undergraduate, occasionally comes to Jewish programs at the university. Rabbi Jack Stein, the Hillel rabbi, knows him by sight. One day, the rabbi receives an email from Denise, a woman who lives far away. The email explains that due to many problems, Denise abandoned her son, Alex, when the boy was a toddler and lost contact with him and the baby's father. Since then, Denise's life has straightened out, and she wants to reconnect with her only child. Through a series of Facebook connections, she found out that Alex attends the university where Rabbi Stein works. In her email, Denise implores Rabbi Stein to please speak with her son and ask him if he would be willing to have contact with his long lost mother.

Questions to consider

1. Would you get involved in this case? Why or why not?
2. How do you decide when to withhold or reveal important information?
3. How does your understanding of your rabbinic role inform your plan for this case?

Discussion

Version #1 (Rabbi Jack decides to call Denise).

Rabbi: Denise, I read your email and gave it a lot of thought. I'm wondering, how did you come to choose me to contact your son?

Denise: I haven't been such a good Jew, but I know that the rabbi is the "go to" person, someone you can trust. I didn't know who else to go to. You are the only one who can help me.

Rabbi: You used the word "trust." I take that seriously. But I'm not sure that I feel comfortable with what you are asking.

Denise: If you don't help me, I don't know if I'll ever be able to contact my son.

Rabbi: Well, what's preventing you from getting in touch with him directly?

Denise: I'm a stranger to him. Worse. I don't have the words. I don't even have the right to barge into his life. But I want to make up for what I did. If you can help me, maybe it can work.

Rabbi: As much as I appreciate your trust, you need to find another way to do this. As the college rabbi, I don't feel that it's my role to intrude into Alex's life.

Denise: I thought I could trust you rabbi. I was wrong. You are turning me away.

Rabbi: I'm sorry.

A central theme in this drama is identifying who is the congregant and then clarifying the rabbi's role. In the above scenario, Rabbi Jack takes a guarded position from the outset. He defines his role as Alex's rabbi only and abstains from assuming a rabbinic role towards Denise or acting as her agent to contact her son. Rabbi Jack feels wrenched by

Denise's story but also manipulated by her request. He does not agree that his participation is the only way for her to connect with her son. Rabbi Jack knows that he could get drawn into the drama of the situation. While he is in a position to help this estranged parent, he feels that he is not the only one who can do so. Denise is not his congregant. Rabbi Jack decides that his primary goal is to protect Alex.

A relevant question here is how the rabbi decides when to excuse himself from a situation. Rabbi Jack wants to let Denise know that his decision has to do with his allegiance to Alex and not disapproval of her. While the rabbi denies Denise's request, he still feels sorry for her. Rabbi Jack decided to call her rather than replying via email. He explains his decision. "My response isn't about if you have been a good Jew, but rather because I don't feel that contacting a student on this campus for what you are asking is something I should do as the Hillel rabbi."

A different pastoral approach might be a scenario in which Rabbi Jack consents to Denise's request. In this version, the rabbi contacts Alex and arranges a meeting with him.

Version #2: (in-person meeting Rabbi Jack and Alex).

Rabbi: Hi Alex. I'm glad you came. Something really unexpected happened to me that affects you. It came through me; you know rabbis can be the "go to" people. This is big news ... I don't know you that well, and this is really heavy ...

Alex: What are you trying to tell me, Rabbi?

Rabbi: This is heavy, and I don't know how true it is, but I received an email from the woman who claims that she is your biological mother.

Alex: My mother ...?

Rabbi: She found out that you are on this campus and wrote to me. She wants to make contact with you and asked me to help her.

Alex: [pause] Why are you doing this? Are you trying to help her or me? It's like a stranger has barged in. She left when I was very young, too little to have any memories of her. My dad raised me. He remarried. I have a pretty decent relationship with my stepmother. I don't want to have anything to do with the woman who sent you the email.

Rabbi: I understand. I thought it was a worthwhile to try. I invited you to come today, so I could tell you that she contacted me.

Alex: I don't even know what to say. I think I need to leave right now.

Rabbi: I see that you are upset … If you can imagine, it was hard for me to decide what to do.

Alex: You agreed to do it. This person is a complete stranger to you and to me. What did you tell her?

Rabbi: I said I would deliver the message. I'm sorry if I upset you. That was not my intention. I felt it was important for you to know that this woman is looking for you.

Alex: Imagine if you were in my shoes. Could you listen to a proxy?

Rabbi: I understand. I wasn't sure what to do, and I made a choice. I told her that I would contact you, but I didn't promise her that either you or I would get back to her because I didn't know how you would feel. I thought you could either find out from me or you would hear from her directly. At least you know now. Here's what I'd like to suggest. If it's okay with you, I'd like to check in with you next week. Even for a few minutes. If your biological mother contacts me again, I will let her know that I gave you the message, and you are thinking it over. I will also advise her to let you make the next move, as there is a lot for you to think about. I advise you to give this a little time to sink in. I'm here if you need me.

Alex: That sounds good.

In this version, Rabbi Jack understands his pastoral mandate as including two congregants, Denise and Alex. This defines his goal, to serve as liaison between an estranged mother and child. The rabbi's mission quickly becomes complicated when he hears Alex's abrupt, upset reaction. Rabbi Jack understands that Alex's first response is to direct his anger towards the rabbi, the messenger. Thus, the rabbi reminds Alex that he, the congregant, is in control of what happens next. Rabbi Jack will facilitate Alex's wishes. Should Denise contact the rabbi again, Rabbi Jack will let her know that he did what she asked and that he advised waiting for Alex to make the next move. Rabbi Jack offers that Denise can keep him updated with her current contact information.

Example 36. An unconventional family in the community

Dr. Ellen Shapiro, the director of the local JCC, receives a kindergarten application for Baruch Price-Spiegel, the four-year-old son of Elisheva and Ronit Price-Spiegel, a lesbian couple. The JCC program is the only Jewish school in town. Dr. Shapiro gleans from the application that the Price-Spiegels also have an infant daughter.

Questions to consider

1.   What is the principal's obligation to this child and family?
2.   What is the principal's obligation to the community?

Discussion

As Dr. Shapiro considers whether to accept a child from a same-sex household, she identifies short- and long-term goals. Right now, the principal needs to deal with whether to accept Baruch into the kindergarten class that begins in a few months. First, she meets with Elisheva and Ronit to explore their expectations and hopes for their son's education. Second, she sets up meetings with the faculty executive committee and the steering committee of the parent association to gauge faculty and parent body reactions to a child from a lesbian household entering the school. This work is time-consuming and demanding. Along the way, Dr. Shapiro contacts colleagues in the Jewish and broader educational community to gather their wisdom and experience as to how they deal with similar challenges.

Dr. Shapiro believes that every Jewish child deserves a Jewish education. While this axiom guides her acceptance of Baruch Price-Spiegel and his little sister down the road, she is also mindful of the protests likely to ensue if a lesbian couple joins the school community. Dr. Shapiro anticipates this latter situation by meeting with a representative group from the school, such as the executive committee. She also inquires as to the couple's experience in joining a local synagogue. If they are members of a congregation, Dr. Shapiro considers that she might garner further support through their synagogue rabbi.

Rabbis and educators are constantly pulled in different directions on controversial matters, many of which are connected to gender and sexuality. Community members' opinions run strong on these topics. In a situation such as this, there is no outcome that will be acceptable to all people. If Baruch is accepted and enters kindergarten, some people will be outraged. They may boycott the school or start a breakaway institution. If Baruch is rejected, other people will protest the exclusion of a Jewish child and oppose the discrimination against same-sex families. The educator's role in this case is to develop support from a broader consensus of the board and larger school community. Dr. Shapiro presents her position in well-reasoned discussions that advocates for educational, religious, and social inclusion of Jews. She anticipates mixed responses that include anxiety, pushback, and support. Her ultimate decision proceeds from this process.

Whether Baruch is rejected or accepted as a kindergartner, Dr. Shapiro has more work ahead. In a climate where rejection of this child is the majority opinion among the board members, it is very important that the educator not absolve herself and the community from the responsibility of providing a Jewish education for Baruch, including finding appropriate tutors. While Dr. Shapiro regrets the decision, she understands that there will be many other issues down the road for the Price-Spiegels in which she can be supportive and helpful. If the decision is to accept Baruch and integrate the family, she plans her strategy for how she will explain the decision to people who may not agree with it. Dr. Shapiro's work is not done once Baruch is enrolled. The administration needs to prepare the faculty and staff with pre-emptive diversity training. Children will ask questions like "Why does Baruch have two mommies?" Ronit and Elisheva Price-Spiegel should be consulted on this. Teachers need to look out for whether Baruch is picked on or excluded by his peers and their families. His parents will need to decide how to participate in school events so that other parents get to know them.

The above scenarios are handled within the framework of pastoral counseling in that clergy act in a pastoral role without making a referral. In all three scenarios, clergy plan some kind of follow up.

• Rabbi Kane recites a prayer for the baby and anticipates visiting the next day.

- Rabbi Jack Stein arranges up a second pastoral interview to check in with Alex.
- Dr. Shapiro sets up a series of meetings with Baruch's parents and key members of the school community.

Other interviews may lead clergy to determine that congregants' situations warrant a level of proficiency that exceeds pastoral training.

Making a referral

When a referral to a mental health professional is warranted, clergy play an important role in bridging the connection. Congregants often resist such referrals. They feel comfortable with their rabbi and are anxious about going to a new person. They express concern about cost or the perceived stigma of consulting a mental health professional. It is important that the rabbi explain how the referral will be helpful as well as how he or she will stay personally involved.

In addition to raising concerns about mental health needs, pastoral counseling also raises issues related to religious and secular law, ethics, and medicine. While clergy cannot achieve expertise in all of these areas, they are responsible for acquiring basic knowledge regarding common conditions and treatments. In addition, clergy need to cultivate mentors who can advise on more complex situations. Such mentors may be teachers from religious or secular educational settings. Clergy might also reach out to people with specific expertise in a niche area. Knowing when to consult senior clergy, a mental health professional, gynecologist, or lawyer, to list a few examples, is key to competent pastoral counseling.

For example, in the case of Matthew Green, Rabbi Marcus does not attempt to treat his congregant's alcohol abuse. Instead, he facilitates a referral to Alcoholics Anonymous or another treatment program. Rabbi Marcus supports Matthew's recovery with regular check-ins and practical interventions, like making sure that grape juice is always available for kiddush in the synagogue. Having become more aware of alcohol problems in the community, the rabbi might go further and ban hard liquor from all synagogue functions. Another situation that warrants referral is that of an acute mental disorder. Recall Example 10, in which the rabbi and his wife detected postpartum depression in a woman who had recently given birth. Rabbi Marcus recognized that his role was not to treat Jane's illness but rather to accompany her along the path of recovery. In this case, clergy best serve the new mother and her family by recognizing her distress, providing practical support such as childcare and meals, and facilitating a referral to a mental health professional with expertise in this area.

When making a referral, the rabbi needs to anticipate resistance. In the case of Lucy, in Example 11, Rabbi Kane felt that the level of the young doctor's religious scrupulousness suggested OCD. The rabbi believed that Lucy deserved a mental health consultation to determine whether this condition was present, and if so, to receive treatment. Suggesting this to Lucy might result in her feeling insulted by being labeled mentally ill. Under such circumstances, the rabbi should not back down from her initial position but rather explain to Lucy that her religious life will be enhanced by clarifying psychological obstacles that distract from full spiritual participation. The next story depicts different manifestations of resistance.

Example 37. The rabbi encounters pushback when making a referral

Brian Schwartz, a 47-year-old married father and a dean at the university who attends services at the Hillel, asks to meet with Rabbi Jack Stein. In the course of their first meeting, Brian discusses his apathy with religious life. At the second meeting, Rabbi Stein discovers that over the past six months, Brian has been smoking a lot of marijuana. Brian claims that this helps him deal with escalating anxiety, depression, and insomnia. He also discloses that he has lost 12 pounds and has difficulty concentrating at work. Rabbi Stein feels increasingly sure that Brian needs to see a mental health professional for evaluation and treatment of his mood disorder and substance use.

Rabbi Stein's goal for their third pastoral counseling session is to refer Brian to an excellent local psychiatrist, Dr. Patricia Johnson. She is a secular Protestant who is respectful of faith traditions. Rabbi Stein got her name when he arrived at the university three years ago from another clergy member of his pastoral peer supervision group. Rabbi Stein explains the referral. Brian balks, making several arguments:

1. "Rabbi, meeting with you has been so helpful. Why can't I just keep on seeing you for a couple more weeks?"
2. "You know how bad our finances are. I can't afford to see some expensive private shrink."
3. "If the university finds out about all the weed I'm smoking, I'll lose my job for sure."
4. "Rabbi, how can you send me to a non-Jew? Don't you care about my spiritual wellbeing?"

Discussion

Making a successful referral requires knowledge, tact, and follow-up. As in the above case, the rabbi must be prepared for the congregant's resistance and to assuage his anxiety. Brian's first response, that Rabbi Stein is doing a great job and so there is no reason to switch, is a frequent argument made by congregants who do not realize that the rabbinic role has a specific agenda, which is support rooted in religious tradition. Pastoral counseling is not designed to provide the long-term depth of mental health treatment. Even if Rabbi Stein also holds a degree in psychology or counseling, he should not provide non-rabbinic professional services for his own congregants. Treating congregants runs the risk of distorting the clergy–congregant relationship. Consider the situation in which a rabbi is also a physician. While he might render professional services for people outside of the congregation, he should not treat a congregant's heart condition. Similarly a chaplain with a law degree refrains from negotiating a congregant's social security benefits or transacting her will. While experience in other fields richly informs clergy's frame of reference, their primary work for congregants must stay grounded in pastoral care.

Clergy need to cultivate a bank of diverse resources in order to make useful referrals. They begin to build their contact list even before arriving in a new community. If possible, an incoming rabbi solicits names of qualified and trustworthy professionals from the outgoing rabbi, as well as from other sources, such as congregants and fellow clergy of other faiths in the community. In the interest of privacy and confidentiality, the rabbi should not refer members of his or her community to other congregants for professional services.

Clergy will have occasion to refer to professionals in private practice, as well as to clinics with sliding fee scales. They will need referrals for congregants experiencing acute psychiatric distress, marital or family conflict, sexual problems, eating disorders, and substance abuse. Rabbis will also encounter situations that warrant legal and financial advice. Certain clergy positions offer built-in referral networks, such as campus settings, where there is a university health service, and military chaplaincies, where other service-related resources are available.

Referral to an expert does not mean that the rabbi abandons the matter. The rabbi considers how to sustain ongoing spiritual and practical needs of people who come for consultation. In cases where the rabbi has a previous relationship with the congregant, such as a member of the synagogue, the rabbi will be in touch about the situation going forward. This ongoing connection again differentiates pastoral care from mental health treatment. In contrast to the therapist, who generally waits for patients to initiate contact, a rabbi might ask a congregant how he or she is doing via phone or email or in person during some natural encounter in the community.

Thus, Rabbi Jack Stein answers each of Brian Schwartz's anxious questions with a response that communicates his pastoral concern and ongoing commitment:

1. "Thank you Brian. I appreciate your confidence in me. I'm not trained in the kind of treatment that you deserve. I want to help you get it. As your rabbi, I want to support you through this time."
2. "I can help you find lower-cost treatment via United Jewish Appeal/ Federation or through the medical school. I want to emphasize that, in my opinion, treatment must be a priority for you."
3. "There is no reason why anyone would find out about your marijuana smoking unless you tell them. From what you've told me, I don't believe that you pose a danger to yourself or anyone else."
4. "I know Dr. Johnson well and have referred other people to her. She is an excellent psychiatrist who is respectful of religious tradition."

As you approach the end of a pastoral interview, ask yourself the following questions:

- Has this interview resolved the situation?
- Are further resources indicated?
- If referral is appropriate, to whom will you refer?
- How will you facilitate the referral?

Following up

Another major distinction between mental health treatment and pastoral care is follow-up. In general, therapists wait for patients to contact them. As described in Brian Schwartz's story, clergy stay involved with congregants over time and have many opportunities to check in regarding all kinds of situations. The following story illustrates how pastoral intervention can fall short if follow-up is not planned at the end of the interview.

Example 38. A student far from home

In October, Steven, a freshman whom Rabbi Jack Stein met at orientation comes up to him on campus. From what the rabbi recalls, Steven appears more serious than the first time they met. He seems to have something on his mind.

Steven is far away from home. Last week, a buddy of his from high school who went to a local college died in a water-skiing accident. Steven tells Rabbi Jack that Jeff was a great guy, kind of off-beat. He had a lot of tattoos and piercings. Steven couldn't go back home for the funeral and feels very sad. He is thinking of getting a tattoo himself.

Steven: Hey, Rabbi, how are you?
Rabbi: Just fine Steven. How are things going for you?
Steven: Classes are okay. But I have a question.
Rabbi: Go ahead.
Steven: What does Judaism believe about the afterlife?
Rabbi: Steven, I can't tell you that on one foot. But tell me, why are you asking me that?

Steven: I don't know …. the truth is, I had a friend, Jeff, who died in an accident last week.

Rabbi: That's terrible. I'm sorry to hear. How are you doing?

Steven: Okay, I guess. I can't go to his funeral. I feel really bad about that. It's too far and costs too much to get there. I've been thinking about getting a tattoo just like the one Jeff had on his right arm, so that I can remember him. But I'm asking about the afterlife because even though Jeff didn't do most Jewish stuff, he was a Jew, and I heard that if you have tattoos, you can't be buried in a Jewish cemetery.[3]

Rabbi: I'm sure it's really hard being far away from home when something like this happens. The question you ask about tattoos is a very interesting point in rabbinic law and one I would be happy to go over with you when we have time. It sounds like he was a really good person and that's what matters. It's hard to be far away from friends and family at a time like this. I can understand why you might want to do something like getting a tattoo in order to help you commemorate Jeff's life. It would be great if you would come by and we can talk about the Jewish view on these and other issues.

Steven: Yeah. Thanks Rabbi.

Steven walks off. The entire encounter is less than three minutes long.

Questions to consider

1. Is this an adequate pastoral intervention for this congregant?
2. How would you end this interview?

Discussion

At the outset of the interview, Rabbi Jack feels worry that a college freshman is asking about Judaism and the afterlife. The rabbi wonders if someone Steven knows is dying or whether Steven himself has thoughts of ending his own life. The rabbi probes the point and notes that the student's manner seems appropriately sad and calm as he explains that his friend died in an accident. Rabbi Jack does not feel a sense of urgency and decides to wait and gather more information in the hope that it will naturally clarify Steven's reason for asking the question.

As the interview unfolds, Steven spells out his worry that tattoos may have negative consequences, even for the dead. Rabbi Jack understands that Steven is reckoning with his friend's death, as well as how to grieve in the context of Jewish tradition. While the impromptu nature of the interaction does not lend itself to a more robust discussion, the rabbi does alleviate Steven's concern for his friend's soul. Rabbi Jack understands that Steven's question is not a request for a complicated, philosophical discussion about either the afterlife or Jewish tradition, which prohibits tattoos. Thus, he focuses on Steven's loss of an old friend and the fact that the student is grieving far away from his home community. The rabbi's goal is to establish contact with Steven and build a rapport that hopefully will grow over time. Rabbi Jack appropriately avoids a pedantic answer regarding the problem of tattoos. At the same time, he recognizes that it takes a lot for someone non-observant to approach him with a religious question. Rabbi Jack recognizes that Steven may feel that his religious questions are unworthy. Hence, this young man might actually feel put down by the rabbi's failure to engage in a discussion of tattoos, as addressing the tattoo question would acknowledge that Steven's question is legitimate.

On the whole, Rabbi Jack does a good job. He avoids the familiar pitfall of over-intellectualization and does not respond to Steven's query with a cerebral or academic response. He also does not feel that Steven needs a referral to campus mental health at the present time and so does not mention this resource. However, Rabbi Jack's conception of his rabbinate is not just to answer an immediate question; he cares that young people connect to Jewish life. While Steven is looking for just this kind of meaning, he is wrapped up in the present and is not thinking about further contact with the rabbi. Unless Rabbi Jack sets up a specific time for their next meeting, he may not see Steven for a long time. In wrapping up the interview, Rabbi Jack would improve his chances of establishing an ongoing relationship with Steve by saying something like, "How about we talk some more next week. Do you have time on Monday?"

In the above example, Rabbi Jack missed the cue to set up specific follow-up. The next scenario further illustrates how missed cues can undermine good pastoral intentions and leave both rabbi and congregant floundering at the end of the interview.

Example 39. An older parent needs help

Ralph and Sheila Klarfeld, a married couple in their early forties and the parents of four young children, are members of Rabbi Kane's synagogue. Sheila's father, Jerry, age 78, lives alone, an hour away, in the house where Sheila grew up. The neighborhood has become unsafe, and Jerry spends much of his time isolated at home. He looks unkempt and poorly nourished. Jerry is a difficult man, critical and moody. He has limited finances. Sheila has two siblings, one who is single and the other who lives overseas. Sheila wants her dad to move in with her, Ralph, and their children, "temporarily." She is home with the children and feels she could look after her dad as well. Ralph's business is precarious. He can barely meet basic expenses. He cannot pay for a fancy senior home for his father-in-law. He calls Rabbi Kane and asks to meet with her.

Rabbi: Come in Ralph. Good to see you. We have around a half-hour to talk. We can decide as we get closer to the end of the time if we need more.

Ralph: Thanks, Rabbi. I'm personally fine. But the real issue is that my wife's father is not in such good shape. Sheila wants him to move in with us.

Rabbi: Tell me more.

Ralph: I don't know how it can work. I did say years ago that we would take care of our parents if they needed us, but I don't think our marriage can survive this.

Rabbi: Having parents move in can really be difficult. Do you get along with your father-in-law?

Ralph: Jerry is a grumpy old guy. He also has high blood pressure and a bad hip. Two years ago my mother-in-law passed away She really took care of him. He has been impossible since.

Rabbi: How does Sheila feel?

Ralph: This was her idea. He lives in a really scary neighborhood and doesn't go out much. He eats terribly. I do believe in honoring our parents, and I want Sheila to be happy, but it's not tenable for our relationship.

Rabbi: I see.

Ralph: I wish we had the money to help Jerry live in one of those nice retirement communities, but we don't. Not with my business in the hole the way it is now.

Rabbi: How does Jerry manage financially?

Ralph: He has a pension from his job and social security.

Rabbi: He doesn't have any personal savings?

Ralph: No.

Rabbi: Have you checked out whether any social services are available that might help him stay in his home? UJA/Federation is a good resource.

Ralph: Not really. Sheila thinks he just has to get out of that lousy neighborhood. It will be really tense with her if we leave him there. While I cringe at the thought of him living with us, I think it's a situation where the commandment to honor our parents comes in. What do you think, Rabbi?

Rabbi: Honoring our parents is an important value.

[Pause]

Ralph: Sheila and the kids could help out. But over time he is sure to deteriorate. Sheila really fell apart with her mother's death. I can't even imagine how she'll handle this.

Rabbi: Have your kids been involved in these discussions?

Ralph: Yes, they like visiting him and seeing his old stuff, but I don't think they understand what having him live with us would be like. Rabbi, are your parents alive? I think I remember making a *shiva* call to your house. I just don't remember right now if it was for your mom or dad, or one of your husband's parents. Did you and Max ever have to deal with a situation like this?

Rabbi: Ralph, we could talk about my family situation, but I don't think that would help resolve your problem.

[Long pause]

Ralph: You know, I think I need to figure this out on my own. I don't want to take any more of your time, Rabbi.

Ten minutes of the session remain. Rabbi Kane feels bad that Ralph has disengaged and wants to leave. She is perplexed about what went wrong in the interview.

Questions to consider

1. What made Ralph want to leave so quickly?
2. Did Rabbi Kane do something wrong?
3. What do you do when you make a pastoral mistake?

Discussion

This pastoral session gets off track early on when Rabbi Kane fails to follow up on the emotional content of Ralph's comment about his marriage not being able to take the strain of bringing his father-in-law into their home. Instead of listening closely to the tone of Ralph's words, Rabbi Kane asks a series of concrete questions about finances and offers problem-solving tips. Doing this causes the rabbi to miss the true source of her congregant's distress – ambivalence about wanting to be a good son-in-law and feeling that it will come at the expense of his marriage.

Rabbi Kane assumes that the goal of the interview is to find an alternate living solution for Jerry. However, when hints of potential marital distress surface, the rabbi should have enlarged the scope of her counseling inquiry and shifted to Ralph's feelings about Sheila, their marriage, and his overall angst about their family finances. Instead of responding to these strains, Rabbi Kane perseverates on Ralph's relationship with Jerry. This is not the main issue. A straightforward question, "What do you think would happen if Jerry moved in?" or a simple, empathic comment, "Tell me more about how you think that would go," would encourage Ralph to explore his ambivalent feelings in a safe, pastoral context without his wife present at this first interview.

Ralph gives the rabbi another chance to open the topic of his and Sheila's strained relationship in his repetition, "It's not tenable for our relationship." Rabbi Kane offers a weak response, "I see." This remark, which under other circumstances might be heard as supportive, feels like a bland conversation stopper. In response, Ralph shifts to a discussion of finance that is more comfortable for the rabbi. Rabbi Kane should have encouraged Ralph to continue talking with a firm, inquiring remark such as, "I see. Tell me more about your and Sheila's relationship."

Rabbi Kane also misses an important religious and psychological opportunity when Ralph poses his question about the imperative of honoring parents. The congregant brings up the Ten Commandments in an effort to speak his rabbi's language. He hopes that Rabbi Kane will reciprocate and listen to him more carefully. However, she brings up an entirely new topic – whether Ralph and Sheila's children are involved in the decision. At this point, Ralph's overt frustration takes over the interview. He bluntly queries the rabbi about her own experience with a parent's death. Ralph's failure to remember which of the rabbi's parents had died denotes his unconscious anger at Rabbi Kane's failure to discern his situation. While readers might debate how much of the rabbi's personal information belongs in the interview, Rabbi Kane's curt response brings the final curtain down on this pastoral interaction. Ralph quits the interview feeling no better than when it began.

Ralph's problem requires more than one pastoral counseling session. The goal of the first interview should be to get an overview of the situation and then establish priorities. While Rabbi Kane identifies at least two main issues, marital strain and Jerry's wellbeing, she fails to address either directly. Helping this family cope with the many issues posed by an increasingly frail, elderly parent will require ongoing pastoral intervention with both Jerry and Sheila.

Making mistakes

As described in the above vignettes, well-meaning clergy, like mental health and other professionals, make mistakes. All clergy need to be prepared for this eventuality. They need to apologize for errors in information, judgment, or technique. When a rabbi says, "I'm sorry. I've been thinking about what I said when we met, and it wasn't right. I'd like to discuss the issue some more," this registers powerfully with congregants. By acknowledging a mistake directly, clergy demonstrate that the fundamental religious response to error is apology and correction. Nothing demonstrates commitment to a congregant more than having the rabbi say, "I was thinking about you" or "I was thinking about our conversation." In contrast to psychotherapy, where a patient would be encouraged to probe the therapist's error as a springboard for deeper inquiry, pastoral counseling is not designed for such exploration. If Ralph, for example, were to return to his inquiry about Rabbi Kane's relationship with her own parents, the rabbi might answer in a general way that conveys useful wisdom, "My experience with my dad's passing made me more aware of how the strained parts of our relationship stay with me." Or "My experience with my mom's later years gave me an appreciation of how much community support means in a time of loss."

Thus, Rabbi Kane might telephone Ralph the next day.

Rabbi: Hi Ralph. How are you?

Ralph Okay, Rabbi.

Rabbi: Do you have a few minutes now?

Ralph: Sure.

Rabbi: I've been thinking about our conversation yesterday.

Ralph: Really. How so?

Rabbi: I feel I missed the boat. I want to apologize.

Ralph: Oh?

Rabbi: Yes. I got all caught up in thinking about your father-in-law's finances. And while that for sure is important, I didn't pay enough attention to the bigger issues.

Ralph: Well, I don't know …

Rabbi: You and Sheila are really trying to do right by Jerry. At the same time, it seems that all the options put a huge strain on the two of you.

Ralph: That's for sure.

Rabbi: I'm wondering if it might be helpful for you and Sheila both to come in and maybe we can put our heads together on this.

Ralph: Thanks, Rabbi. I appreciate your calling back on this. I'll talk to Sheila and let you know.

Rabbi: Great. I'll check in with you next Wednesday if I don't hear from you before then.

Table 5.1 Key principles of the pastoral interview.

Listen actively	Establish and maintain an alliance with the congregant. Stay in tune with one's own emotional pulse.
Assess urgency	Is there any danger? Does the situation require emergency intervention?
Establish the frame	Define appropriate time and place for the interview
Acknowledge congregants' needs	What does the congregant want or need?
	What is the rabbi's role in this situation? What guidance can be drawn from religious tradition?
Develop initial hypothesis	Stay alert for information that supports or changes first assumptions. Be prepared to revise initial hypothesis as more is learned.
Establish a hierarchy of goals	What needs to be taken care of right now? What can wait?
Sum up and make a plan	Does this interview address the situation sufficiently? Is another meeting indicated? Are other professional resources called for? How will the rabbi follow up?

Notes

1 If a man has an affair, there are no halachic consequences for his marriage. In contrast, if a woman has an affair, under certain circumstances, she and her husband would be halachically required to get divorced.

2 A woman who has sexual intercourse (defined as vaginal or anal intercourse) with a man who is not her husband is prohibited from remaining married to her husband. There is little to no halachic latitude if two witnesses directly witnessed the woman having sex with another man (see Rema, Shulchan Aruch Even Ha'ezer 20:1 for specifics). In the absence of witnesses, she is prohibited from remaining with her husband only if she claims that intercourse took place and he chooses to believe her (see Shulchan Aruch Even Ha'ezer 115:1). Some halachic authorities provide solutions that can be found in such circumstances (see, for example, Rema, Shulchan Aruch Even Ha'Ezer 178:9, who states that we reject the husband's statement that he believes his wife that she committed adultery on the grounds that he may be looking for an excuse to remarry). In this case, when she is not sure if she engaged in intercourse, the husband and wife would almost certainly be permitted to remain married.

3 Tattoos are prohibited according to biblical law (see Leviticus 19:28 and Shulchan Aruch Yoreh Deah 180:1). Halachically, a person with a tattoo may be buried in a Jewish cemetery, just as it is permitted to bury people who have committed other sins.

Chapter 6

Preparing for the unexpected

Clergy must be prepared to deal with unconventional and surprising situations. These include requests for counseling that fall outside the conventional rabbinic sphere or that involve people outside the rabbi's usual sphere of congregants. Clergy must also be prepared for unexpected and powerful feelings that come up for congregants and for themselves, even in routine interview situations. The best preparation for unexpected situations or feelings is having a clear sense of the rabbi's role, as well as knowledge of one's own emotional responses and how to respond to them.

Responding to requests for counseling outside the conventional rabbinic scope

What is the rabbi's responsibility, if any, to people who are not his/her congregant or part of the regular community that the rabbi serves? What are the expectations for clergy in terms of providing pastoral care to people with whom they will not have future contact? This question becomes more complex when the rabbi finds him/herself negotiating situations in which pastoral involvement is unsuitable or even contra-indicated. For example:

- A man sits next to the principal of a religious school during an airplane flight and contacts her through Facebook a week later. He asks if she knows of any drug rehabilitation programs that are sensitive to spiritual needs.
- A rabbi gives a lecture in a distant city. After the question and answer period, a woman in the audience comes over and asks the rabbi whether she is obligated to provide financial support to a sibling who defrauded her years ago and is now destitute.

- A person in prison asks the chaplain to bring a package to a friend in the community.

Because people view clergy as obligated to help all people in times of need, a rabbi is bound to find him/herself in such situations. This may include help for trivial matters and consequential crises. Clergy cannot solve all problems for all people. But how does the rabbi determine which situations warrant involvement? How does a rabbi walk away from requests for help that are inappropriate or beyond the scope of rabbinic care?

The first step with non-congregants is to assess the urgency of the situation. When clergy make such a determination, their responsibility is to help direct the person in need to the appropriate resources. More often than not, the situation is not urgent. In these cases, clergy are most helpful by answering straightforward religious questions and directing the individual to local resources for further support. Thus, in the above examples:

- The principal emails her seatmate from the plane and suggests an organization that she has read about. She also advises him to contact his local Jewish family services organization and community mental health resource to inquire about suitable rehabilitation programs.
- The rabbi validates the audience member's dilemma by acknowledging the tension between family responsibilities and helping someone with a history of offensive behavior. The rabbi explains that the situation deserves more discussion than the rabbi can provide and encourages the woman to meet with local clergy.
- The chaplain explains that the rules of the institution prohibit chaplains from conveying any materials in or out of prison.

In all three cases, clergy need to be wary of the sense of specialness evoked by such situations. As described earlier, people in need often endow clergy with unreal expectations and power that exceed their actual capacities. Some clergy feel that it is a noble responsibility of their religious vocation to try and resolve all situations that come their way. However, most often, clergy are far more useful when they provide a level of service appropriate to a limited interaction. Clergy do not help acutely distressed people when they initiate a level of involvement that will not likely be sustained. In fact, an intense pastoral intervention that is abruptly discontinued can feel like abandonment and re-traumatize a person who has already been through a painful time. It is more helpful to connect distraught individuals to social or therapeutic networks, which will both help them solve their immediate problem and also provide the skills and support needed to sustain them over time in the broader community. Often, clergy provide the most aid when they refrain from trying to solve the problem on their own and instead connect people in trouble to professionals who can offer tailored, ongoing support.

A vignette illustrates how clergy can become involved in a situation in an indirect, but positive, way.

Example 40. The rabbi's grandmother has a friend in need

During Rabbi Jack Stein's visit to his grandmother, Rhonda Stein, she asks him to say a blessing for her friend's son, Boaz Fink, age 57, who is critically ill. Rabbi Stein has never met Boaz or his family. Boaz dies a few days later, and Mrs. Stein's friend, Arlene Fink, calls Rabbi Stein to ask if he would officiate at the funeral. She explains that her son was not affiliated with any formal religious community and that they do not have a family rabbi. They would like the funeral to be Jewish, but they "don't want any religious stuff."

Questions to consider

1. What issues come up for you when friends or family ask you to perform clergy functions?
2. How do you respond when the request is for a vague "Jewish" presence?

Discussion

In this case, the request for rabbinic service comes from two different people, Rabbi Stein's grandmother and her friend. Rabbi Stein's experience has taught him that funerals are a powerful life-cycle event and an opportunity to connect families to Jewish heritage. He feels that the Finks' request falls within the parameters of his rabbinic function, and he has some free time. He agrees to perform the funeral. If he were not able to do so, he would have helped the Fink family connect to local rabbinic resources.

Rabbi Stein meets with the family and asks, "Tell me what you had in mind when you called me. I'm a traditionally observant rabbi and conduct funerals a certain way. I want to find out what kind of Jewish funeral would be meaningful to you. I want to check in with what feels right and what doesn't feel right for you." Rabbi Stein tactfully offers some education about Jewish customs, "Let me walk you through things." He explains basic protocol of preparation for burial, graveside ritual, and *shiva*.[1] The Fink family agrees to a traditional burial and an abbreviated *shiva*.

Rabbi Stein debates with himself as to whether he should charge a fee for his services. He decides to do so for two reasons. First, rabbis generally charge for performing funerals. Rabbi Stein will spend several hours preparing with the family and then conducting the funeral. Second, his impression is that the Finks have a positive feeling towards Jewish ritual. He hopes that this experience comforts them during their loss and connects them to further participation in Jewish tradition. He understands that payment is a way for people to acknowledge value and express gratitude.

Responding to an unusual request

Sometimes clergy are asked to provide services that are outside their conventional scope of practice or training. For example:

- A congregant asks the rabbi to officiate at a nephew's wedding in another state.
- Parents grateful for the services of a hospital chaplain during their son's two months in the neonatal ICU ask the chaplain to perform their baby's circumcision.

Regardless of the decision they make, clergy should be upfront and clear. If a rabbi chooses to decline a request, the rabbi explains the reason for doing so. If possible, the rabbi directs the person to appropriate alternate resources:

- In responding to the request that he perform the marriage, the rabbi might reply, "Thank you for asking me. I will decline because the demands of my schedule make it difficult for me to do the job that is required. When I perform a marriage, a lot of counseling goes into it. While I wish the young couple much happiness, I think it's better for them to find a local rabbi." The rabbi might then go on to suggest a specific rabbi or direct the congregant to resources for finding local clergy.

- The hospital chaplain might respond, "Thank you so much for this honor. While I am thrilled that your son is strong enough for his *brit milah* and touched by your request that I serve as *mohel*, I am not trained in this technique. I can suggest someone else who I know is excellent." Depending on availability, the chaplain might offer to be present and participate in the *bris* in some fashion.

When the request for pastoral involvement comes from a third party

Another challenge faced by clergy occurs when a pastoral situation involves a third party. Congregants concerned about the health or welfare of loved ones may ask clergy to intervene when they do not know what to do or are worried that confronting the situation directly will jeopardize their relationship.

Example 41. Distressed parents want the rabbi to intervene

Claire Lerman calls her family rabbi, Daniel Marcus, and asks that he make an intervention with the Hillel rabbi, Jack Stein, where her son Aryeh attends college. Over Thanksgiving, Aryeh came out to his family as gay. Claire and her husband Keith are devastated. They feel it is urgent that their son receive religious and psychological help with this problem as soon as possible, but the Hillel rabbi does not seem to share their opinion.

Questions to consider

1. Should a rabbi reach out to a third party at the request of a congregant?

2.   Would you contact the Hillel rabbi based on Claire Lerman's phone call?
3.   Would it make a difference if you had a prior relationship with the Hillel rabbi?
4.   How do you provide pastoral counseling to different sides in a difficult situation?

Discussion

As he listens, Rabbi Marcus realizes that Aryeh is going through a life transition and that his parents are very distressed. The rabbi understands that the purpose of Claire's phone call is to recruit his help in reorienting Aryeh's sexuality by speaking with the campus rabbi. Rabbi Marcus does not share her goal. He has not been in touch with Aryeh for some months and does not know whether Aryeh feels that his sexuality is a problem or whether he needs professional mental health intervention.

Rabbi Marcus feels that he should not intervene with Aryeh or with the rabbi on campus unless Aryeh initiates a request for such consultation. While he has met Rabbi Jack Stein before, he does not contact him to discuss Aryeh Lerman without permission from Aryeh. At the same time, Rabbi Marcus understands that Aryeh's parents experience their son's announcement as a crisis. The rabbi invites Claire and Keith to come and talk. He explains that an issue of such magnitude deserves discussion in person. His goal for the meeting is to preserve family bonds as they all grapple with the new reality. If they agree to come in, part of his counsel will be to offer his availability to meet with them and Aryeh, together or separately.

Another kind of challenge encountered by clergy involves receiving indirect information that suggests serious misconduct on the part of other congregants or fellow clergy.

Example 42. An allegation of improper behavior

Nancy, a 43-year-old married congregant, calls Rabbi Kane and tells her that Gail, an 18-year-old high school senior who occasionally babysits for Nancy's children, confided disturbing information. Scott, a married man and member of the synagogue whose children Gail also babysits, has been flirting with Gail over the past several months. Gail told Nancy that Scott recently suggested that Gail accompany him on an overnight business trip in a few weeks. Nancy adds that her babysitter seems excited by Scott's attention.

Rabbi Kane informs Nancy that she needs to speak with Gail directly about the situation. She counsels Nancy to let Gail know that Rabbi Kane will be getting in touch with Gail about the situation. Nancy reluctantly agrees. Rabbi Kane is aware going into the conversation with Gail that she may be exaggerating or even lying. Their subsequent talk leads her to believe that the young woman is credible. She decides to intervene.

Questions to consider

1. How do you balance confidentiality with concern about potential harm?
2. How do you define your responsibility for congregants' ethical behavior?

Discussion

In this difficult situation, a third-hand allegation seriously impugns several congregants' reputations. The rabbi draws support from established protocol. Throughout each step of her intervention, Rabbi Kane checks in with her feelings. She recognizes that she feels anger and disappointment related to Scott and confusion in relation to Nancy. Rabbi Kane also wonders if Nancy is jealous of Scott's attention towards the attractive teenage babysitter. Rabbi Kane is aware that this swirl of emotions could easily tilt her into hasty action. She needs to proceed carefully. This means listening to each person's story and getting permission to share material before going further. Thus, in her conversation with Nancy, Rabbi Kane thanks her for coming to her. She asks Nancy what concerns she has and how she would like the rabbi to be of help. Nancy answers, "Well, Rabbi, I just thought you would be the right person to stop this situation before a lot of people get hurt." Rabbi Kane informs Nancy that in order to do anything, she must speak directly with Gail. Rabbi Kane asks Nancy's permission to do so. Rabbi Kane understands that oral communication constitutes a kind of personal property. Just as she would not borrow Nancy's property without permission, so too she cannot use the material she has confided in her without express consent.

If Nancy gives consent for the rabbi to proceed, Rabbi Kane sets up a meeting with Gail. The rabbi opens the meeting by telling the young woman that Nancy has given her permission to discuss a serious matter. After sharing what she knows, the rabbi asks Gail for her side of the story and listens to see whether it is consistent with Nancy's version. If the rabbi surmises that the accounts indicate inappropriate behavior on Scott's part, she advises Gail to sever her relationship with Scott. Rabbi Kane also tells Gail that she plans on having a conversation with Scott in which she will express her concern for Scott and the welfare of his family. If Nancy does not give Rabbi Kane permission to divulge the story, the situation changes. Rabbi Kane will likely feel frustrated, as though Nancy has dumped a problem on her but deprived her of the ability to even attempt to solve it. If Nancy refuses to allow Rabbi Kane to go forward, the rabbi's challenge is to work with Nancy on understanding her reasons for disclosing the story. She needs to recruit Nancy's cooperation in order to get consent to talk to Gail or make any further intervention.

If Nancy refuses to give permission, Rabbi Kane must be on the lookout for any feelings of disappointment or anger that she has towards her congregant. An important component of clergy work is maintaining pastoral alliances even when thwarted by congregants who refuse to collaborate on difficult matters, such as whistle-blowing. Clergy are in the unique position of having multiple points of contact over an extended period of time. The ability to maintain compassion and patience in the face of frustration serves well in forging alliances that support painful but necessary interventions.

Thus far, this section deals with managing the content of communication between clergy and congregants. The next section describes the multiple modalities of communication that mediate pastoral encounters.

Dealing with different forms of communication

Direct interactions offer valuable non-verbal information through facial expression, body language, and subtle shifts of tone. Sitting across from the rabbi also informs the congregant's pastoral experience as he/she receives counterpart messages through the rabbi's non-verbal communications. In reality, however, a great deal of pastoral counseling is initiated and conducted via phone calls or a variety of electronic modalities. Under extenuating circumstances, face-to-face contact might not be possible. These include students living away from home or congregants who are traveling. For example, if Aliza or Aryeh spend a semester abroad and encounter a situation that they want to discuss with Rabbi Jack Stein, email or Skype might provide the opportunity for the Hillel rabbi to formulate an initial impression, help a student through an acute difficulty, and, if needed, make a referral to a local pastoral counselor or mental health professional.

Clergy need to be thoughtful about the use of different forms of communication. This is especially true because any contact other than a face-to-face interview leaves a permanent record and the vast potential for communication to be disseminated in cyberspace. Clergy should assume that all material, whether text message or email, will reach the eyes of multiple readers. People regularly forward communications onward without adequate consideration. In general, confidential or sensitive material should not be shared online. Care should be taken with any electronic communication. Clergy should not send any electronic communication that expresses their gut reactions without appropriate reflection beforehand. Oftentimes, a few hours' delay results in a more neutral, nuanced presentation of the same issue.

While phone messages, texts, or email may efficiently answer simple questions from congregants, they fall short of addressing more serious inquiries. If a congregant emails to ascertain whether a certain food is kosher, the rabbi can write back with reasonable confidence that he/she has provided an adequate response and not missed some underlying pastoral need. However, clergy need to be alert to the possibility that even seemingly simple questions can veil more complex issues.

Example 43. A text request raises concern

Rabbi Marcus receives a text from Simone Green, "Can you recommend a good divorce lawyer?"

Questions to consider

1. Would you respond by text?
2. How do you choose when to text, email, or call?

Discussion

Rabbi Marcus does not text back contact information for a matrimonial attorney. This is especially true if this is the first time he is hearing about divorce in the context of Simone's life. Rather, he calls Simone back, acknowledges her text, and probes the situation further. Depending on the situation, his efforts may be met with a wide variety of responses.

- "Oh, thank you Rabbi for your concern, this is for my sister-in-law. Matthew and I are doing much better!"
- "I'm really worried about my friend; her marriage is in terrible shape, and I feel like I've neglected her over the last few months while my mother-in-law has been so ill."
- "Things have been going downhill between Matthew and me for a long time, but I didn't have the heart to do anything while his mother was dying."

Consider the following criteria for email, texting, and other electronic communications:

- Use such communications for the purpose of imparting objective information or for scheduling purposes rather than for complex, nuanced ideas that can be misinterpreted.
- Do not feel pressured to respond immediately to any communication.
- Be especially careful with provocative emails or texts.

- Always wait several hours before pressing "send" on any strongly worded email or text response of your own.

These guidelines apply regardless of the nature of the material. They are especially important when dealing with content that raises intense feelings for the rabbi.

Responding to the unexpected

Clergy need to be ready to hear material that is distressing or surprising. It is helpful to anticipate that when a congregant makes an appointment, he or she may disclose material that is new or unexpected. The rabbi's job is to provide a safe, hospitable environment and listen to whatever comes up in an interview. The rabbi must be ready to deal with both the stated reason for the visit as well as any issues that appear to lie beneath the surface.

Example 44. The congregant starts to cry

We return to Example 32, the scene of Rabbi Marcus's interview with Matthew and Simone Green. Simone has blurted out her statement that Matthew's drinking is excessive. The Greens sit far apart on the couch in Rabbi Marcus's office and look straight ahead. Simone begins to cry. She apologizes through her sniffles and takes a tissue from the box of Kleenex that the rabbi keeps on the table in anticipation of such occasions.

Questions to consider

1. How do you feel when a congregant gets upset?
2. How do you offer comfort in situations of distress?

Discussion

This situation might suggest that Rabbi Marcus offer some words of comfort. In fact, he provides far more support by sitting quietly and attentively. His patient, non-flustered interest communicates his availability to hear the material that Simone has bottled up.

Earlier, we described basic space and privacy requirements of the rabbi's office. The physical set-up of the office also contributes to or detracts from an atmosphere of receptive equanimity. For example, consider a seating arrangement in which two chairs of very different proportions face Rabbi Marcus's desk. When a couple enters this room, the decision as to which spouse gets which chair starts off the interview with a potential power struggle. By comparison, if the rabbi's study features similar chairs or a couch, both spouses are accorded equal status.

Body language also communicates a great deal in emotionally laden moments. In the above story, Rabbi Marcus thinks about the simple act of handing a tissue to a tearful congregant. He is mindful that this gesture has subtle potential to undermine the counseling. In a counseling session, the offering of a tissue may be interpreted as indicating the rabbi's desire for the congregant to muffle words as well as tears. In fact, the opposite is true; effective counseling opens channels for feelings that are often released in tears. The pastoral goal is to unpack material, however it is expressed. The rabbi's most helpful contribution is to actively listen and let whatever is going on unfold. Further, in the context of meeting a couple, the rabbi's handing over a tissue or other material to either party might be interpreted as taking sides.

The pastoral response to tears is to acknowledge that deep feelings have been evoked. Rabbi Marcus hypothesizes to himself that Matthew and Simone's marital issues date back some time. He anticipates that new information is forthcoming. The rabbi plans his next comment. He wants Simone and Matthew to pause and investigate the moment that elicited strong emotion. Rabbi Marcus says, "I see that this topic is very upsetting," or "Something just happened. Can you tell me what that is?" By stating what might seem obvious, Rabbi Marcus permits and validates an emotional response. Most importantly, he conveys that he is capable of dealing with anything that is expressed to him. His pastoral hospitality opens the way to further dialogue. Often, a congregant who begins to cry apologizes for being emotional. Again, the most useful counseling response is to resist consoling the crying person and instead treat the expression of tears as a form of communication of important information.

A common but nonetheless surprising pastoral experience is when the problem for which the congregant ostensibly sought consultation gives way to an entirely different problem. Rather than feeling caught off-guard, the rabbi understands that what appears to be a kind of bait-and-switch actually represents the congregant's faltering attempt to get help. Rabbi Marcus sits quietly and observes how the interview evolves. Simone repeats her earlier critique, "It's his drinking, rabbi! Haven't you seen how much scotch Matthew knocks back at kiddush? And that's not all. He's been getting drunk on weeknights as well." Simone turns to Matthew and continues, "The real problem is you, Matthew. If you weren't getting tanked every night, maybe you wouldn't have gotten into so much trouble at work, and our son wouldn't be dropping out and wasting his potential."

Now Matthew looks like he is about to burst into tears. Rabbi Marcus was not aware of Matthew Green's problem with alcohol. He wonders whether Simone is exaggerating. He wonders what else might be going on between Simone and Matthew. Rabbi Marcus checks in with his own emotional pulse and notes that he feels a low-grade agitation that reminds him of the way he felt when his own parents fought during his childhood. He identifies his impulse to soothe and make things better. This helps him stay calm rather than flood the interview with words or scramble for a hasty solution. Rabbi Marcus wants to inquire about Matthew's drinking in a way that maintains neutrality and demonstrates commitment to both congregants. At the same time, he does not want to lose sight of the original complaint that brought the Greens to see him. "I don't want to shortchange the official reason for your visit, your concern about Avi. But now I'm getting the picture that more is going on. Today is the first time I'm hearing about alcohol being an issue. Please tell me more about this." Such a response comes across as appropriate and calming. It demonstrates that the rabbi is not overwhelmed by unexpected material but rather is prepared to receive whatever the congregant confides.

Clergy will hear material that is shocking. When this happens, the best response is to keep the pastoral space calm and to stay emotionally available even in the face of terrible news. The rabbi's response will be important to the congregant, who is likely struggling with whether to speak further. It is useful to pay attention to when in the interview the shocking material comes up. If highly charged material is brought up at the outset or early on in the interview, this might be a kind of test to see how the rabbi will react or what kind of position the rabbi will take. More commonly, the congregant brings up disturbing information towards the end of the session when time is running out. This may indicate avoidance, a behavior common when dealing with painful content. At the same time, bringing up difficult material late in the interview may signal a congregant's wish for the rabbi to prolong the interview. The rabbi makes a judgment call as to whether extending the time will benefit the congregant and also if it is practical for the rabbi's own schedule. Most often, scheduling another meeting will work. There will be cases, however, which warrant immediate attention and additional time. We offer an example.

Example 45. A routine hospital visit takes an unexpected turn

Rabbi Jack Stein pays a hospital visit to Richard Black, age 63, a physics professor who occasionally attends Hillel services and is generally a friendly and positive person. Professor Black has complications from advanced kidney disease. As Rabbi Jack walks into the room, he sees that Professor Black is in bed and appears weak and ill. Rabbi Jack greets his congregant, "It's good to see you, Professor Black. I hope that it is okay if I pay you a short visit, around ten minutes." Professor Black nods. Rabbi Jack takes a seat in a chair next to the hospital bed and attempts to engage his congregant in conversation. Professor Black barely responds to any of the rabbi's polite queries about how he is feeling. The rabbi sits quietly until the end of the stated time. As Rabbi Jack prepares to leave, he asks Professor Black if he would like to say a prayer together. Richard Black answers, "Yes, pray that I will die soon. I've had enough, and I've decided to stop dialysis."

Questions to consider

1. What do you do when a congregant is silent during a visit?
2. How do you respond to shocking revelations?
3. What feelings come up for you when no solution is in sight?

Discussion

Rabbi Jack is startled by what he has just heard. Although he needs to get back to his office for an important meeting, he decides that Professor Black's situation constitutes a pastoral emergency, since discontinuing dialysis will result in death. Rabbi Jack says, "If it's okay with you, I'd like to stay longer and talk more about this. I'm going to text my colleague that I'll be a bit late."

Rabbi Jack continues, "I understand from what you have just told me that you are going through such a hard time that you think you don't want to live anymore." Rabbi Jack looks directly at Professor Black as he says these words and then stops talking. He sits quietly and maintains eye contact. After what seems like hours, but is actually less than a minute, Richard Black begins to speak, "I've been rejected as a candidate for a kidney transplant. I'm just going to die slowly on dialysis." Professor Black continues speaking for a few minutes longer. He voices fears of increased infirmity, pain, dependency, and, worst of all, becoming a burden to his family. Rabbi Jack listens attentively. At one point Professor Black becomes quiet and looks at him intently. The rabbi murmurs, "I'm here for you," after which the older man continues talking.

The divulgence of difficult material is often followed by silence on the congregant's part. Rabbi Jack finds it hard to tolerate what feels like echoing, dead space. He knows that he feels anxious and a little panicky. However, the capacity to hold silence is an important skill. Silence is not inactivity. Resisting the impulse to rush in with words, staying quiet, and letting a story unfold exudes a peaceful power that yields important information.

Rabbi Jack knows there is no easy solution for Professor Black's bleak medical future. He understands that fear and isolation compound his congregant's suffering. These painful feelings likely affect the professor's decision-making capacities. The rabbi offers a simple statement, "I hear how painful and hopeless this feels for you. I'd like to help." Rabbi Jack neither tries to talk Richard Black into wanting to live nor chastises him for talking about ways to end his suffering. The challenge for clergy is to resist feeling responsible for fixing all situations. Instead, the goal is to create a plane of alliance in which clergy can offer comfort, support, and religious wisdom. Rabbi Jack contributes best by staying in the room and absorbing Professor Black's words. Perhaps, if the ill man feels that the rabbi understands his raw and angry feelings, he will feel less desperate and accept interventions that lessen the intensity of his suffering. These might include further visits, prayer, and practical suggestions. While he listens, Rabbi Jack wonders if psychiatric consultation and medication might be beneficial. He makes this suggestion to Professor Black, "I'm also wondering whether your doctor has asked for a psychiatric consult. In my experience as a chaplain, I've seen people with serious medical conditions have a better quality of life with anti-depressant treatment. I want you to be sure that your decision to stop dialysis isn't being influenced by depression that could be treated."

Here are some guidelines for dealing with surprising or revelatory information.

- Your best initial response is silence until you are ready to formulate a helpful reply.
- Check your impulse to rush in to "solve the problem."
- Remember that your presence in itself is a powerful and healing intervention.

Sometimes, as in the vignette above, the congregant pauses and does not respond to the question right away. Novice clergy find this silence hard to tolerate. If the congregant does not answer the rabbi's question at all, this might indicate several possibilities: the question hit a deep emotional place, the question is premature, or the question is on the wrong track. It does not mean, however, that the rabbi should not have asked the question. Sometimes the congregant's silence prompts the rabbi to repeat the question or change the topic. In the rabbi's attempt to avoid gaps of silence or lapses in conversation, the rabbi may fire off a second question. It is important that the rabbi resist the impulse to ask additional questions. A useful acronym to keep in mind is W.A.I.T.: "Why Am I Talking?" As discussed earlier, an uncomfortable silence is often the precursor to a difficult disclosure by the congregant. Therefore, it is vital that the rabbi give the congregant time to respond even if it leads to questions that the rabbi does not know how to answer.

Asking questions

Attentive listening and judicious use of words empower clergy to guide interviews without interrogating their congregants. As described in the above story, fewer words go further. Still, while active and compassionate listening is bound to elicit a great deal of information, clergy will need to formulate questions that encourage pastoral encounters to deepen. These queries should be well articulated and have a specific purpose. Vague, poorly formulated, or excessive questions can derail the purpose of the visit. Questions should be asked one at a time. Bombarding with multiple questions will confuse the congregant and may prematurely close down the conversation because a fusillade of questions indicates anxiety or a lack of pastoral training on clergy's part.

Questions serve multiple purposes in the interview. A goal of pastoral counseling is for clergy to engage congregants in a jointly participatory process regarding the issue at hand. The rabbi generates hypotheses that make sense of a congregant's dilemmas and listens for information that supports or refutes those hypotheses. As the rabbi listens to this material, the rabbi's personal history, experience, and imagination give rise to new ideas. These inform the rabbi's comments that in turn invite the congregant to explore further. Besides obtaining information, a well-phrased question serves to rouse the congregant's curiosity and enlist him or her as co-investigators in their situation. In contrast, a rigid question and answer pattern may polarize the interview by setting up the rabbi as the authoritative expert rather than as a pastoral collaborator who explores the dilemma with the congregant. In short, a narrow question closes down the interview, a double question confuses, and a "why" question not only implies judgment or disapproval but may be impossible to answer. By contrast, a reflective question encourages the congregant to explore more deeply (Benjamin 1981). Consider the different kinds of questions that might emerge in Rabbi Jack's interview with Professor Black.

- "Don't you know how much your family cares about you?" prompts a rigid "yes" or "no" answer. "I wonder if you have had a chance to discuss this with your family" opens the way to deeper dialogue.
- "How can you even consider stopping dialysis?" puts Professor Black on the defensive. "Can you tell me a little bit more about

how you came to this decision?" is more spacious and gives Rabbi
Jack and Professor Black greater opportunity to explore issues.
- "Why haven't you talked to a psychiatrist?" feels like a criticism,
while "Have you considered speaking to a mental health professional?" demonstrates respect for the congregant's judgment.

Clergy often worry that asking loaded questions will put ideas in a
congregant's mind that were not present before. For example, a few
days later in peer supervision over the phone with a classmate from
rabbinical school, Jack Stein reviews his visit with Professor Black.
"Professor Black told me that he feels so bad about how little he can
do and what a burden he has become. He wonders if his family would
be better off without him. I thought of asking him if, in addition to the
idea of stopping dialysis, he has thoughts of actively ending his life.
But I worried that I would be putting the idea of suicide into his head."

In fact, the opposite is true. Bringing up hard or forbidden topics
actually offers relief by communicating that no topic is off-limits in
the pastoral encounter. When Rabbi Jack invites Professor Black
to spell out difficult feelings or thoughts, he signals interest in the
details of the situation as well as his familiarity with the repertoire
of human suffering. Rabbi Jack will not be shocked by what he
hears. The rabbi's availability to listen to unconventional material
does not mean that he condones religiously transgressive behavior.
Rather, his goal is to create a bridge into Professor Black's pained
isolation and help him consider a wider range of choices.

Clergy often incline their efforts towards soliciting information by
posing direct questions. However, the art of interviewing is to subtly
guide a conversation so that information is disclosed naturally. In the
next vignette, tactful inquiry into a congregant's motivation for religious
transition sets the tone for organic unfolding of important information.

Example 46. Exploring interest in conversion

Edward Parker, a law student born to secular Christian parents,
comes to meet Rabbi Jack Stein at the university Hillel office with
his Jewish girlfriend to talk about converting to Judaism. Rabbi
Jack is interested in learning how Edward's interest came about.

Questions to consider

1. How do you evaluate a potential convert's background, motivation, and stability?
2. What feelings come up for you in situations of religious transition?

The first question that Rabbi Jack wants to ask Edward is, "Why do you want to convert to Judaism?" He holds back, realizing that a "why" questions will likely set up an inhospitable and interrogatory tone. Rabbi Jack considers two alternatives formulations for his question.

1. "Which faith tradition were you raised in, and how does your family feel about your interest in converting to Judaism?"
2. "Tell me more about your interest in Judaism."

Discussion

The first option raises two important points. However, a double question that queries Edward's religious background together with his family's stance towards his potential conversion diminishes the opportunity to explore either issue sufficiently. The second phrase invites Edward into collaborative exploration. The invitation to speak openly ("Tell me about ...") also allows Rabbi Jack to see how Edward organizes his thoughts. His responses will guide Rabbi Jack on how to proceed with the interview.

Clergy involved with people contemplating conversion do well to consider the congregant's background, family, and motivation for change. Whatever direction a person's spiritual path takes, it is important to recognize that religious transition, especially conversion, shakes the foundations of an individual's identity and can be quite destabilizing. The journey goes best with a pace that allows sufficient time to integrate the diverse components of the experience. The rabbi serves an important role by guiding a person contemplating conversion to assimilate and process each step. This applies to various groups of people, including those who change religions or become more or less religious in relation to how they grew up. Conversion and transition within religious traditions often generates palpable discomfort, either because clergy themselves have gone through religious change or, if they have not, they may feel challenged by the issues generated by congregants who have.

Back to Edward and Rabbi Jack. Aware that a romantic relationship is involved, Rabbi Jack probes Edward's motivation and commitment to Judaism beyond pleasing his girlfriend. The rabbi avoids language that might come across as accusatory. Rabbi Jack goes on to explain that he has a dual rabbinic responsibility, as a gatekeeper for the Jewish community and as a chaperone for Edward's individual religious journey.[2] Rabbi Jack addresses both obligations by advising that Edward proceed slowly as he takes on religious observances. Edward agrees and asks Rabbi Jack to mentor him in his exploration. The rabbi suggests some books and a course of study. They meet regularly over the next few semesters to discuss Edward's progress.

The next vignette shows how a well-placed question can open up the discussion of another sensitive and often avoided topic.

Example 47. Newlywed distress

Seth and Irene Franklin, ages 24 and 23, married eight months ago. Grievances that seemed small at the beginning of their marriage have escalated, and they fight frequently. They agree to meet with Dr. Ellen Shapiro, who co-taught their marriage preparation class with a rabbi. They each present a litany of grievances. Seth complains that the house is a mess and that Irene insists on spending every holiday with her family. Irene protests that Seth has reneged on his promise to share domestic tasks and that he seems more interested in hanging out with his friends than being with her. Dr. Shapiro notices that they sit at opposite ends of the couch in her office and appear uncomfortable with each other. After listening quietly for 15 minutes, Dr. Shapiro comments, "These are all important issues in day-to-day life. I also notice that neither of you has brought up your intimate life. In my experience, that's often a sensitive topic for newlyweds. I wonder whether you two want to talk about this as well?"

Questions to consider

1. How comfortable are you initiating questions on topics that have not been brought up?
2. Are you prepared to talk about sex and other sensitive topics?

Discussion

Dr. Shapiro demonstrates one way to inquire about a sensitive topic. She neither assumes that there is a sexual problem nor worries whether she is on the right or wrong track. Rather, her choice of phrase, "In my experience ..." communicates awareness that sexual difficulty often contributes to marital distress. Her tone and wording also indicate her comfort talking about the topic with couples. Dr. Shapiro does not specify whether her knowledge comes from pre-marital preparation with couples or personal experience. As discussed earlier in Chapter 3, disclosing personal history as the source of clergy's wisdom is more likely to distract congregants than contribute to pastoral success.

Dr. Shapiro watches Irene and Seth's body language as she listens to what they say. She notes to herself details such as who speaks first, shifts in demeanor, and whether they look at each other. If they disclose that they are having sexual problems, and she has some training in this area, she asks if they are comfortable talking more with her. She is also prepared to refer them to a sex therapist. As discussed in Chapter 5, clergy do a great service when they make referrals. The success of congregants such as Irene and Seth connecting to a therapist will depend a great deal on the skill and tact with which Dr. Shapiro prepares them.

Physical contact

The definition of acceptable social touching between the sexes, whether it is a hug or a peck on the cheek, is not consistent among clergy, regardless of gender or denomination. To some degree, the extent to which a rabbi touches congregants will be determined by denominational affiliation as well as personality style. For example, most Orthodox male rabbis will avoid physical contact with women and girls, including even a handshake.[3] Clergy from all denominations express warmth and comfort to congregants in a wide variety of ways. Whatever their style, clergy should carefully examine personal practices of social physical contact. Rabbis need to consider that congregants of either gender may have different reactions to being touched. Some people do not feel comfortable being embraced by their rabbi. Congregants of both genders might find differential treatment of each gender off-putting; they prefer that their rabbi be an equal opportunity hand-shaker, hugger, or cheek-kisser, or else not touch anybody at all.

"Quick! Remind me—are they handshakers, huggers, single kissers, or kissers on both cheeks?"

Figure 6.1 *New Yorker* cartoon.

Further, the very nature of pastoral counseling lends itself to boundary blurring. Disclosure of personal information may lead to a transient but powerful sense of closeness that slides into physical intimacy. The realm of boundary crossings and violations often begins innocently with disclosing personal information or the confession of deeper feelings between clergy and congregant. While revelation of private material may originate in a well-intentioned attempt to empathize or even empower a congregant, such behavior blurs boundaries and is not advisable. One of the steps that invariably precede inappropriate physical contact is a sense of special emotional closeness between the rabbi and congregant that originates in shared disclosures. Clergy should thus be alert and cautious to avoid trekking into this volatile emotional territory with congregants, regardless of how compelling, enticing, or "safe" a congregant may be.

Most clergy believe that the sanctity of their vocation together with personal discipline protects them from sexual boundary violations. It is for precisely this reason that clergy must understand just how easily this boundary can be crossed. Physical contact often begins with experiences of shared empathy. A useful tip in identifying risky precursors to impropriety is when clergy deviate from previously established norms of religiously and socially acceptable touch. In other words, rabbis need to pay extra attention when they feel that a particular experience warrants a level of physical contact outside their usual repertoire of behavior. Of course, there are times of great emotion when a congregant is so overwhelmed with strong feeling that he or she spontaneously hugs or clutches the rabbi. While tact and compassion should guide the rabbi in such circumstances, confusing feelings may be aroused in the rabbi as shown in the next story

---

Example 48. The rabbi feels uncomfortable and stumbles

Rabbi Marcus has known the Roth family since he came to the synagogue seven years ago. Esther Roth, now age 38, is a charming and attractive woman. When her husband, Simon, was diagnosed with an aggressive brain tumor two years ago, the rabbi grew closer to the family. Simon died ten months ago and was mourned by the whole community. For Esther, life the past two years had been a roller coaster. Taking care of Simon and their three children while trying to keep her career afloat drained her completely. Rabbi Marcus had been such a great help. He was patient, supportive, and thoughtful. He was also attractive and reminded her a little of Simon before he got sick. Esther hopes that the rabbi can give her some advice. She recently met a very nice divorced man in her single parents' support group. Esther asks Rabbi Marcus if they might meet in the morning after nursery school drop-off.

> **Esther:** Thank you for making time to see me, Rabbi. I know I've taken up a lot of your time.
>
> **Rabbi:** That's fine, Esther. I'm happy to be of help. I have around 20 minutes before I have a committee meeting. Tell me, how are you doing?

Esther: It's been hard. It seems like there are always new things, new feelings, new issues that come up.

Rabbi: Of course.

Esther: I don't feel comfortable talking with anyone about this but you. There's really no one else as sensitive or as understanding. You've been so good to me.

Rabbi: We've known each other for years. I would do the same for anyone in our community.

Esther: I know. That's what makes you such a great rabbi.

Rabbi: Many other people in the community helped out also.

Esther: Right. But now my friends are not being so helpful … Rabbi, I need to task you a question. Do you think there's anything wrong with my dating?

Rabbi: Based on the way you're asking me, Esther, it seems like you think there might be. I get the feeling that this is not just a theoretical question.

Esther: Well, last month, I met a really nice man in the single parent support group I joined. He asked me out for dinner. I told two of my friends, and they acted like it was the most terrible thing in the world.

[Esther starts crying]

Simon has been gone ten months, and he was really sick for a whole year before … Really Rabbi, am I such a horrible person for wanting some male attention or affection that isn't connected to cancer?

Rabbi: Of course not.

Esther: So what do you think, it's okay, right?

Rabbi: You might think about this a bit more.

Esther[crying]: You probably also think I'm a bad mother, wanting to go out on a date when my children's father isn't dead a year … You just don't want to say it.

[Esther slumps into her chair, weeping. Rabbi Marcus leans forward in his chair. Esther pulls herself forward to embrace him in a full frontal hug. Rabbi Marcus hugs her back for a second and then drops his arms. He moves further back and speaks.]

Rabbi: You are in a rough place Esther, and I want to be here for you. But we need to stay in words.

[Esther sits back down, takes a tissue, and blows her nose.]

Esther: I don't know, Rabbi. I feel like a huge idiot. I can't believe that I lost it like that. But it did feel good that you hugged me.

Rabbi: I want to continue talking about you and your situation. I think dating would be different in a few months.

Esther: Oh, I'm so happy to hear that. Actually I'm just so happy that you are talking to me. I thought that I had really blown our relationship by hugging you.

Rabbi: [Glances at his watch and is startled to discover that it is minute 18 of the interview.] Let's make it clear. We're talking about you dating the fellow from your group.

Esther: That's what we're talking about.

Rabbi: We had a difficult moment just before. We both know that our relationship has to stay within certain boundaries ...

Esther: Yes! Of course! Why would you think otherwise?

Rabbi: Well, I'm glad you spoke with me about this, Esther. And I'm glad that you met a man whose company you enjoy. Keep me posted.

Esther: Thanks for your time Rabbi. I'll be going now. Say hi to Leah for me.

Questions to consider

1. What are your general guidelines for physical contact with congregants?
2. When do you break those rules?
3. How do you recover from a lapse in your regular protocol of physical contact?

Discussion

This awkward interaction illustrates a classic stumble caused by anxiety. Rabbi Marcus's clumsiness comes from not knowing how to re-establish his role after slipping up. As the scenario evolves, Rabbi

Marcus feels less sure as to what Esther wants. He wonders whether she harbors romantic feelings for him. A better response to Esther's question about dating would be to frame an answer in terms of the rabbinic issue and then make room to explore the feelings generated. This would validate Esther's wishes for companionship and intimacy from the perspective of religious tradition and also set a clear pastoral counseling tone. Rabbi Marcus might say, "If you're asking me from the perspective of Jewish law, it is permitted for a widow to date after three months.[4] I feel that you're also asking me if this is okay for you and your family. We can talk about that more." Instead, Rabbi Marcus's original suggestion that she wait ("You might think about this a bit more") without any explanation conveys a tone of disapproval.

Boundary issues also play a part in the rabbi's discomfort. Rabbi Marcus is flattered by Esther's admiration and idealization. He is not aware that his directive to this emotionally vulnerable congregant to "wait before dating" has a slightly destabilizing effect on Esther, who might perceive both a hint of romantic interest in his manner and also judgmental feelings. Rabbi Marcus is not prepared for Esther's impulsive embrace and even less for how much he enjoys it. While he quickly retreats from her hug, he remains flustered. His sudden awareness of how little time is left in the session adds to his agitation. In his discomfort, he makes the mistake of prolonging the conversation about what just happened rather than letting it go and moving on to the stated reason for Esther's visit. That is, his statement, "Let's make it clear … We had a difficult moment just before," accentuates Esther's embarrassment and confusion.

Had Rabbi Marcus not leaned forward and presented Esther with the opportunity for any physical contact, the situation might have been averted. However, once Esther responds to his gesture in a manner that was beyond his conscious intention, Rabbi Marcus's job is to extract himself from the embrace and re-establish conversation. Such behavior protects the emotionally vulnerable congregant's dignity. It also shields the rabbi from acting on tender, even romantic feelings that he may not have been fully aware of until that moment.

It is neither necessary nor desirable for the rabbi to discuss the matter further. If Esther brings up the incident, for example, to apologize,

Rabbi Marcus tactfully acknowledges the duress of the moment and reassures her that their pastoral relationship is intact. This is unlike psychotherapy, where the therapist–patient relationship is deliberately cultivated as a proxy to explore dynamics of the patient's life. While these dynamics also hold true for pastoral encounters, the rabbi's goal is not to probe for deep psychological motivation but to guide the congregant pastorally. After Esther apologizes for her behavior, Rabbi Marcus simply says, "That's okay, Esther, I understand."

Physical contact conveys many possible meanings. In the above example, Esther's behavior is not motivated in the main by a wish to seduce the rabbi. Some congregants want to initiate romantic involvement with the rabbi. Some rabbis exploit moments of vulnerability and physical contact as opportunities for seduction. In all situations, clergy bear the primary responsibility to re-establish appropriate boundaries. We suggest:

- that you establish your own guidelines for physical contact for both genders;
- when protocol is breached, take the lead in restoring proper boundaries.

Notes

1 Basic restrictions of *shiva* include not going to work, not leaving the house for pleasure-related purposes, not sitting on chairs of a normal height when others are present, not bathing for pleasure, not anointing oneself, not wearing leather shoes, not engaging in sexual relations, not learning Torah, not greeting other people, not laundering clothing, not shaving (for men) or getting haircuts, and not wearing *tefillin* (phylacteries) on the first day (see Shulchan Aruch Yoreh Deah 380). For practical guides to Jewish mourning, see Lamm 1969, Goldberg 1991, and Drucker 1996.
2 The rabbi has a responsibility to ensure to the best of his/her ability that the convert is sincere and to make sure he or she understands and accepts the responsibilities of being Jewish (see Shulchan Aruch Yoreh Deah 268:2, 12).
3 According to Jewish law, for anyone with whom sexual relations are not allowed, affectionate contact of any kind is also forbidden (see Rambam, Hilchot Issurei Biah 21:1, Shulchan Aruch Even Ha'ezer 20:1, 21:7). There is a debate whether neutral touch, such as handshaking, is likewise forbidden. Rabbi Moshe Feinstein prohibits handshaking as too affectionate (Iggrot Moshe Even Ha'ezer 4:32.9), while Rabbi Yehudah Herzl Henkin permits such neutral touch (Benei Banim 1:37; this position is also widely quoted in the name of Rabbi Joseph B. Soloveitchik). Many adopt a middle position, forbidding it as a rule of thumb but permitting it in cases where it would cause embarrassment or discomfort.

4 In fact, according to Jewish law, she may date sooner than that. She may not remarry until three months after her husband's death (Shulchan Aruch Even Ha'aezer 13:1).

References

Benjamin, Alfred (1981). *The Helping Interview* (Boston: Houghton Mifflin).

Drucker, Reuven (1996). *The Mourner's Companion* (Highland Park, NJ: Ramat Gan Publications).

Goldberg, Chaim Binyamin (1991). *Mourning in Halachah* (New York: Mesorah Publications).

Lamm, Maurice (1969). *The Jewish Way in Death and Mourning* (New York: Jonathan David Publishers).

Chapter 7

Establishing and maintaining confidentiality

Privacy and confidentiality

At the outset, it is important to distinguish privacy from confidentiality. Privacy refers to what people share about themselves with others and how they establish environments in which information is revealed. Earlier in this book, we gave guidelines for pastoral contact that include preparing physical surroundings for and paying attention to the timing and length of interviews. In addition to maintaining a respectful and dignified environment, these protocols protect the privacy of people who consult clergy. Confidentiality is an extension of privacy. It refers to the treatment of information that has been disclosed in a relationship of trust. Confidentiality is built on the expectation that material disclosed will not be divulged to others without express permission.

In the United States, pastoral counseling in each state has been codified as a "clergyman–penitent privilege" that presumes that clergy will not disclose any information confided by a congregant. This default assumption does not provide for situations in which Jewish law calls upon a rabbi to disclose information that has been told in confidence (Broyde, Reiss, and Diament n.d.). Consider a 2001 New York state court ruling in which an observant woman in the process of divorce sued two rabbis for violating her confidentiality by disclosing to her husband that she no longer observed laws of ritual purity (Schaffer 2005). The court held in favor of the defendants, the rabbis. Orthodox Jewish law requires that a woman perform ritual immersion after completing her menstrual cycle and before she re-engages in sexual activity with her husband.[1] The New York state ruling recognized that the rabbis had a religious duty to protect the spiritual wellbeing of the husband and was acting within their rabbinic vocation to protect him from committing a serious violation of Jewish law which would have occurred had he engaged in prohibited sexual relations with his wife. While the rabbis won the above court case, they failed in their pastoral role by not disclosing to the congregant that they had an obligation to reveal material told in confidence that they deemed to be of potential spiritual harm to her husband. It is important to consider how the rabbis could have avoided this failure.

It is essential that clergy clearly communicate their definition of confidentiality. Clergy should not make blanket promises to keep secrets. The best approach is for the rabbi to tell congregants that conversations are not absolutely confidential when the rabbi senses that the conversation is approaching dangerous territory. This way, the congregant can make an informed decision about how much information to reveal. In the case of the woman telling the rabbi that she was having relations with her husband without going to the ritual bath, the rabbi should have said something to this effect before finding out anything definitive that he would be obligated to relate. A more general statement might have been, "By coming to me you are asking for my help. You are probably assuming that everything you say to me is confidential. You don't have to tell me about your private life, but if you have stopped going to the *mikvah*, then you have a religious and moral obligation to inform your husband, and I would fully expect you to comply with that religious obligation." The rabbi might add, "You know that having sexual relations without going to the *mikvah* is a problem. From a religious point of view, you are causing harm to your husband. I am also responsible for protecting your husband against religious violations." By making these kinds of statements, the rabbi communicates that while disclosures of behavior that pose physical or spiritual danger to the congregant or others are not protected, the rabbi respects the congregant as a partner in the counseling enterprise and pledges to keep non-harmful material confidential.

Best practices for rabbis include knowing state guidelines for clergy confidentiality, procuring liability insurance, and participating in risk management programs that consider both religious and secular legal perspectives. Confidentiality also includes safeguarding private information. Examples of private information are:

1. A change in health status. Rabbis should not say prayers out loud on behalf of an ill person unless they have explicit permission from that person to divulge the fact that the person is ill.
2. A change in marital status. Rabbis should not divulge engagements, separations, or divorce to anyone without express permission.

It is important to adopt strict guidelines about privacy. Documents containing names or other identifiable information must never be left on a desk or in a location where someone else can see them. Conversations about other people should always be conducted outside of the audible range of casual bystanders.

If the rabbi believes it is important to share congregants' emails or other communication, it is essential that congregations grant him or her permission to do this. The rabbi must obtain permission before divulging any personal information about congregants.

Many congregants are concerned when they first come to see the rabbi about whether and to what extent confidentiality will be maintained. When congregants ask about confidentiality, clearly explain the parameters under which your counseling can take place

Clergy need to be familiar with secular legal statutes that frame clergy–penitent privilege and should note that these laws vary by state. As described in the story recounted above, a rabbi, unlike a therapist, may feel obligated to intervene in a situation of perceived spiritual danger. Similar situations include learning that someone is spreading slander or that a merchant is selling non-kosher products as kosher.

Example 49. Confidentiality and mental illness

Rabbi Shira Kane receives the following email from Oren Kole, an occasional visitor to the shul.

> Hi Rabbi,
> I just wanted to drop a quick line. I'm sorry that I've missed services in the last few weeks. I'm trying to work on my relationship with Lana and would like your advice …
> I have one more year of probation left from when I passed some bad checks. Lana doesn't know about any of this. As a condition of my probation, I am required to see a therapist.

My therapist asked me whether I was afraid that I might pass on my bipolar genes to the baby I plan to conceive with Lana. I asked her later not to say things like that to me and compared her, along with my overtly anti-Semitic probation officer, to Nazis who would have euthanized and sterilized people like myself. She asked me to find another therapist. This endangers my probation.

Lana doesn't know that the courts believe I have a mental illness because, of course, I do not agree with them. But she is more secure and grounded in our relationship than ever. She asked for a specific timeline to have a baby. I suggested June of next year when my legal problems will be resolved, without explaining the reason for this date. Lana has agreed. If you have time to talk about these issues, I would be very appreciative.

Questions to consider

1. Do you feel a concern about how much Lana does or does not know about Oren's psychiatric status?
2. Do you feel it is your obligation to make sure that Lana is informed?
3. How do you feel about people with major mental illness having children?
4. Would this situation seem different to you if Oren had a significant physical illness, rather than a psychiatric one, that he had not disclosed to Lana?

Discussion

Rabbi Kane reads this email over several times. She writes back to Oren, thanking him for his trust, and asks that, given the important topics in the email, they meet in person. The rabbi notes that she feels an immediate surge of protective concern for Lana, whom she has not met. She wonders how much Lana knows about Oren's history and whether she is aware of what Rabbi Kane presumes is his chronic level of paranoia. As Rabbi Kane sits with these feelings, she considers that the couple has been together for two years, during which Lana has had time to become familiar with aspects of Oren's character and history. Lana is responsible for inquiring about Oren's past and making decisions about his suitability as a partner. In Rabbi Kane's brief encounters with him, Oren has been pleasant and cooperative. The rabbi decides to craft her pastoral response around these more immediate issues. Rather than email her response, she invites Oren to meet.

In their meeting, Rabbi Kane conveys that Oren is a valued member of the community and that Lana is most welcome to come to the synagogue. Their conversation continues.

Oren: So what did you think about the rest of what I wrote?

Rabbi: I'm glad you brought this up. I know you don't have to tell me those private things. I feel good that you trust me and that you care about Jewish values.

Oren: That's right, Rabbi. So what do you think?

Rabbi: Let me just check in. Which matter do you want to talk about first?

Oren: About the plan to have a baby together.

Rabbi: Well, I believe that a couple making a serious life commitment need to have honesty between them about the big things. Like health and trouble with the law.

Oren: [bristling] Rabbi, I told you that Lana doesn't know this stuff. This is all going to be gone by next June. Promise me that you won't tell her.

Rabbi: I will keep what you confided in me private until you give me permission to do otherwise or I am seriously worried about your or someone else's health or safety. But I know from experience that big secrets have a way of coming up. I'm also hoping that the two of you will marry before having a child, and I would be honored if I could work with you both in pre-marital counseling. How about you think about this? In the meantime, I'd like to see more of you, and I hope to have more of these conversations.

Rabbi Kane should not discuss Oren's legal or psychiatric problems with Lana or anyone else without Oren's permission. Rabbis often feel helpless if they cannot divulge what they feel is pertinent information to someone else. Even when working with a couple, the rabbi has an obligation to maintain the privacy and confidentiality of each spouse. This need not result in pastoral paralysis. In the event that there is a real fear of loss of life or other serious physical danger that could result from non-disclosure, clergy need to reconsider. For example, if Rabbi Kane felt that Oren might be a danger to himself or someone else, she might call and alert his therapist, who, as a mental health professional, is best able to determine whether a real danger exists and what further action is necessary. The next example focuses on the complexity of counseling both members of a congregant couple.

Example 50. The rabbi counsels a distressed spouse

Laura Harris calls Rabbi Marcus to set up an immediate meeting to discuss problems in her marriage. She comes in and immediately asks, "Rabbi, everything I say stays between us, right?" Rabbi Marcus nods his agreement. Laura goes on to describe in great detail her husband's escalating verbal abuse toward her and their children. Rabbi Marcus suggests that he meet with Laura and her husband, Richard. Laura says she will think about it and get back to the rabbi.

A few weeks after the meeting with Laura, Richard asks to meet with the rabbi. Richard's normally cheerful manner shifts to sadness as he describes Laura's erratic behavior at home with their children and her sudden refusal to have sex. Rabbi Marcus listens but does not reveal that he previously spoke with Laura about the state of the marriage. A short time later, Laura tells Richard of her meeting with the rabbi. Richard calls Rabbi Marcus and accuses the rabbi of betraying his trust by not disclosing that he had already met with Laura.

Questions to consider

1. How would you respond to Richard's accusation?
2. What would you have told Laura when she asked you about confidentiality?
3. Under what circumstances should a rabbi agree to keep secrets?

Discussion

Rabbi Marcus missed several red flags in this case. First, he should not have let Laura assume that he could maintain blanket confidentiality no matter what the circumstance. Second, in a fractious situation where verbal abuse is alleged, the rabbi neglected to investigate the possibility of physical abuse and determine whether Laura or the children were in danger. Finally, as a congregational rabbi serving both members of a married couple, Rabbi Marcus is also Richard's rabbi. The rabbi should have advised Laura that in the event that Richard should ever come to him, Rabbi Marcus would need to disclose the fact that he had a previous conversation with Laura. Depending on the circumstances, Rabbi Marcus might suggest that she inform her husband that she had a conversation with the rabbi. While Rabbi Marcus could provide assurances that he would keep the details of their meeting private, he needed to anticipate the possibility that Richard might also come to talk about the troubled marriage. Points that emerge from this discussion are:

- Do not be too quick to assure confidentiality.
- When you are counseling a member of a couple or family with whom you have a relationship, remember that you are the rabbi to all parties.

The value of confidentiality extends to the clergy couple. Congregants have widely divergent expectations of their rabbi's spouse. For example, community expectations often include that rabbis and their spouses host festive meals and teach classes. Congregants may look to the rabbi's spouse for pastoral advice. Some who do so will assume that information told to him/her will be relayed to the rabbi, while others may expect that conversations with the clergy's spouse will be held in confidence. On the clergy side, the situation is also complicated. After a long day, a rabbi might or might not look forward to discussing challenging pastoral matters with his/her spouse. Rabbis need to apply rigorous standards of confidentiality to pastoral communications with their spouses as well. Clergy couples need to discuss this with each other and consistently inform congregants of their confidentiality standards. Even if the rabbi's spouse is a mental health professional, the rabbi should not discuss specific privileged material with his/her spouse without express permission from the congregant. There are numerous reasons for this, as highlighted by the following stories.

Example 51. A casual dinner conversation

During a Hanukkah meal at the university, Ellie Bach, a junior, sits next to Rabbi Jack Stein's wife, Miriam, a high school math teacher. Over dinner, their conversation turns to students' experiences of transitioning to college. Ellie confides that since her mother's recurrence of breast cancer two months ago, she has been struggling with her own faith and religious practice. Miriam listens and responds, "I understand how your mom's illness would really be challenging for you. I'm glad that you came to this Hanukkah dinner and trusted me with this confidence. Would it be okay with you if I discuss what you've told me with Rabbi Jack? I know he cares, and I think he could help you work this through some more."

Questions to consider

1. How does your spouse handle pastoral communications?
2. What are your practices as a couple regarding confidential information told to one of you?

Discussion

Miriam Stein's natural talent for listening to people has been honed in her work as a teacher and her role as a Hillel spouse. While this dinner conversation functioned almost as an initial informal counseling session, Miriam feels that Ellie would benefit from further discussion with her husband, who has more experience dealing with religious explorations during crisis situations. She does not assume either that Ellie is telling her about her religious struggles with the intention that Miriam will pass this along to the rabbi or that she has permission from Ellie to disclose these confidences at all. Thus, she spells out her request to share Ellie's concerns with her husband.

Example 52. The rabbi keeps a secret from his wife

Leah Marcus runs the local community day school. The job involves both academic and business functions. Leah has been looking for an executive director for several months, but the limited salary offered for the position hampers the search. Just this week, Matthew Green, a high-powered executive and member of the synagogue, approached her about the job. Matthew explained that he had been laid off from his company due to the economy. During his interview at the school, Matthew said that his dream was to work for the Jewish community. Leah is thrilled with this stroke of luck and can barely wait to talk with her husband, Rabbi Daniel Marcus, about Matthew later that evening.

Recall that Rabbi Marcus has learned, over the course of several pastoral counseling sessions with Matthew and Simone Green, that Matthew has a serious drinking problem and has been let go from his position as chief financial officer due to his erratic attendance record and diminished performance. Matthew's company was willing to say that they were downsizing his position.

That night over dinner, Leah happily relates that she has finally found the perfect person to fill the job of executive director at the school.

Rabbi: How was your day?

Leah: Great! We had a real breakthrough at school.

Rabbi: With the executive director job?

Leah: Yes! The right person just walked right in. Matthew Green. You probably know his story. He lost his job – downsizing. Matthew says he has always wanted to give serious time to community service. It's a little sooner than he expected, but this could be perfect.

Rabbi: Amazing that it just happened like that. What are you going to do next?

Leah: We are obligated to do the regular background check, references and all that. But I figure that you know him well.

Rabbi: Matthew is a terrific person. He has a lot to offer. I think you want to be very sure about this … especially because he's a member of the community. If it doesn't work out, it will be difficult.

Leah: Hmm, is there more going on then you're saying? Do you know something you want to tell me?

Rabbi: Well …

Leah: I'm feeling like the air has just been let out of my balloon. You're not being helpful here, murmuring caution but not telling me what's wrong.

Rabbi: I can't say Matthew isn't right for the job. On the contrary, I would say that he has impressive credentials. I just think you want to apply the same criteria to him as you would to anyone else.

Leah: Really, Daniel. This job affects the whole community. Don't you think you should tell me what you know?

Rabbi: You're not wrong. What I can tell you is to make sure that you go through the proper channels. Actually, I may have crossed the line right now. I didn't mean to rain on your parade.

Leah: Okay, I get it. I should have picked up your cue that this is something confidential. Just tell me straight next time. I'll take it from here.

Rabbi: You're right. I imagine that you have had situations in school where parents ask you not to tell me something about their kid or their family. We should just spell this out to each other when it comes up. Thank you for understanding.

Leah: It's hard sometimes, not being able to talk about this part of our work.

Questions to consider

1. What do you do when confidential information you learned in a counseling session directly impacts other people in your life?
2. How does keeping secrets affect your closest relationships?
3. How do you resist the impulse to share information?

Discussion

Daniel and Leah Marcus struggle with this provocative situation. The rabbi's goal is to ensure that the confidential information in his possession will not affect his wife's protocol in this job search. His unintended, more cryptic message was to warn her to be especially careful. Some readers might find his behavior to be like a wink, as though he is saying, "I can't really tell you, but ..." They would prefer that the rabbi tell his wife earlier in the conversation that he cannot talk about the subject. An approach might be, "I really apologize, but I can't participate in this conversation. Let's talk about something else." Another perspective is that the "duty to warn" factor applies more vigorously in this case. But concerns for protecting the community, while admirable, must be evaluated with great care. As with cases of alleged impropriety, proper channels and confidentiality must be respected. At this point, Rabbi Marcus does not have information that indicates that Matthew's alcohol use poses danger. The rabbi is actively working to help Matthew get treatment. Thus, while Matthew Green's active alcohol abuse was the reason he lost his corporate position, Rabbi Marcus should not interfere in his congregant's job search.

Clergy and spouses need to revisit the topic of confidentiality throughout their vocational lives because their practices and policies are sure to be tested many times. Confidentiality imposes a special strain on clergy marriages that is distinct from those of mental health professionals. While therapists are also obligated to maintain professional confidentiality, the psychologist would not treat a friend or acquaintance and thus is far less likely to acquire information that has direct impact on his/her spouse or family. Active and open communication in the clergy couple is critical. The couple must set guidelines for these issues early in their relationship and revisit them over time.

Allegations of boundary violation

The topic of confidentiality also extends to handling boundary regulations and alleged infractions. Rabbis, educators, and other Jewish professionals are often the first to hear about claims of impropriety, especially when it comes to sexual matters. Clergy, as discussed earlier, may also be accused of boundary violations. These stories quickly become notorious and lead to fractured communities and widespread distress. In this section, we stress how important it is for clergy to proceed according to clear and calm protocol when investigating any accusation of impropriety.

Example 53. A disturbing report

Leah Marcus and a congregant, Bella Sasson, spend an evening together in the synagogue assembling welcome packages for new congregants. Bella, a 42-year-old divorced mother of two and the art teacher at the community day school, is an active member of Rabbi Daniel Marcus's congregation. As the two women chat, Bella confides to Leah that Cantor Raphael Porath, who is married and has children, has been behaving in a way that makes her uncomfortable. Leah asks Bella to explain. Bella describes that the cantor commented that a dress she wore recently "shows off her figure really well." She also feels that he lingers around her unnecessarily. One night last week he asked if he might drive her home after an arts program at the school. Bella declined the ride, and Cantor Porath seemed very disappointed and even a bit angry. Bella adds that she heard another woman joking about how Cantor Porath seems more interested in her than in her son's bar mitzvah lessons. Later that night, Leah says to her husband, "Daniel, you have to do something about Raphael. He really is out of line."

Questions to consider

1. What criteria do you use to evaluate potential harm?
2. How do you handle situations when congregants have not given you permission to investigate or confront disturbing behavior?

Discussion

This situation suggests inappropriate boundary crossings by Cantor Porath. Note that while none of the cantor's behavior involves physical contact or involvement with minors, it evokes discomfort and serves as fodder for rumors. If minors were involved, mandatory reporting, required by United States law in most states, would be invoked. In this case, Rabbi Marcus feels concern both for his congregants and the cantor. He has known Raphael Porath for several years and considers him a friend. He wonders if Bella is exaggerating or has some other agenda in confiding in Leah.

Rabbi Marcus's immediate goal is to have a tactful but firm conversation with Cantor Porath. However, he realizes that the allegations were not told directly to him and, at this point, are hearsay. Daniel Marcus checks with his wife as to whether she asked Bella if it was okay to repeat to him material told to her in confidence. Leah replies that she isn't sure. Rabbi Marcus asks her to please call Bella and ask for permission. Leah does so and explains to Bella that this is a topic of great concern and that she believes her husband needs to know so that he can address it properly. Bella agrees.

Rabbi Marcus calls to arrange a meeting with her and goes over the story. He asks Bella for permission to have a discussion with Cantor Porath about his behavior. Bella becomes worried. She is afraid that the cantor will recognize her as the source of the story and retaliate. She is a single parent, and Cantor Porath is well liked by the community. She might lose her job. Rabbi Marcus is not successful in persuading Bella. While he is disappointed, he directs his efforts into bringing in a staff consultant to review boundary awareness for the entire synagogue clergy, staff, and the community day school faculty.

Rabbi Marcus acted correctly. Too often, people who learn of potential boundary infractions worry, "What will happen next if we don't stop it now?" Their anxiety about the future gets in the way of taking care of what is going on at the moment. In order for an allegation of potential misconduct to be substantiated, firsthand evidence must be gathered. This requires building trust with people who make claims, a process that may take time. Of course, knowledge of possible misconduct will influence a person's attitude towards the alleged perpetrator going forward. Rabbi Marcus will be watching Cantor Porath's behavior much more carefully from now on. At the same time, the rabbi also must be mindful about showing prejudicial behavior towards Raphael Porath or Bella Sasson. In other words, with allegations of impropriety, individuals are presumed innocent until proven guilty.

If an allegation of impropriety crosses secular or religious legal lines, such as physical involvement with a minor, illicit drug use, or sex with a married woman, Rabbi Marcus would have taken a more aggressive stance. When facing situations of alleged misconduct, it is important for clergy to have clear protocols to follow and also to have legal consultants and religious advisors to go to for guidance. In many states, clergy are mandated to report suspected abuse of minors. To ensure compliance with the law, all religious institutions should designate a committee of laypeople, such as board members, with whom confidential discussions can be had regarding worrisome boundary behaviors. A reporting and investigative structure needs to be in place for synagogues, schools, camps, JCCs, and other institutions. These protocols should be linked to clergy governance bodies, such as rabbinical organizations across the denominations or organizations such as Hillel, camp movements, or United Jewish Appeal/Federation. In addition, these organizations need to make ethical standards and repercussions of impropriety explicit to their members.

Note

1 The Torah prohibits sexual relations between a man and a woman during menses and for several days thereafter (Leviticus 18:19, 20:18). She remains in this state until she immerses in a *mikvah* (ritual bath) (Shulchan Aruch Yoreh Deah 195:1).

References

Broyde, Michael, Yona Reiss, and Nathan Diament (n.d.). "Confidentiality and Rabbinic Counseling: An Overview of Halakhic and Legal Issues," www.jlaw.com/Articles/RabbinicCounseling1.html, accessed June 30, 2016.
Schaffer, Sylvan (2005). "Rabbinic Confidentiality," in Yisrael Levitz and Abraham Twerski *A Practical Guide to Rabbinic Counseling* (Jerusalem: Feldheim), pp. 342–356.

Chapter 8

Working in groups

Until now, our discussion has focused on fundamentals of pastoral counseling in the context of one-on-one interactions between clergy and congregants. In this chapter, the same principles of active, compassionate, non-judgmental listening; awareness of transference/counter-transference dynamics; attention to structuring pastoral interventions; and confidentiality are applied to group settings. Clergy often counsel families, lead groups, and organize activities. While these activities are quite different, there are similarities in the dynamics evoked. Group work involves authority, delegation, and mediation, and conflict management is a core element in successful group work.

Clergy's work with groups invokes a different level of spiritual authority. Rabbis generally function as the group leader, rather than as an equal participant. It is useful to distinguish between the methods and goals of mental health professionals and clergy regarding group work. Mental health professionals will recommend group therapy when they feel that patients will benefit from peer feedback. In group therapy, the therapist's role is to help the group notice and interpret longstanding behavioral patterns, communication styles, and interpersonal dynamics as they arise. Pastoral counseling group work is different, because clergy's job in a group is to resolve more immediate situations without necessarily interpreting meaning or motivation. Instead, clergy utilize an understanding of group dynamics to facilitate religiously relevant goals. In considering group process, it is also important to remember that clergy, in contrast to mental health professionals, have multiple spheres of social interaction with congregants. For example:

- A rabbi meets with members of a blended family to plan a wedding.
- A camp director facilitates a staff discussion about new educational programming.

• A chaplain convenes a meeting with a patient's family members and ICU staff to discuss a matter of medical ethics.

The family serves as a helpful basic template to understand group dynamics. The family is both a unit unto itself and also a collection of individual members. Generally, within each family, different members take on different roles (MacKenzie 1990). Groups of all kinds tend to organize along similar lines. These groups often include the social member who emphasizes positive interaction, the structural member who is concerned with task accomplishment, the divergent member who challenges the status quo, and the cautionary member who holds back and is wary of group process. As in a family of any composition, various members of a group fill organizational and emotional roles that may or may not conform to gender stereotypes. Someone, usually the father or mother, but possibly a grandparent or older sibling, functions as the designated leader. Either that same person or someone else is the unofficially designated nurturer, healer, organizer, worrier, or troublemaker.

The challenge in working with families is that it is not always clear which member is functioning in which capacity. Think about the question of a telemarketer, "May I speak with the head of the household?" The answer to this question is not always easy. Usually, the telemarketer refers to the head decision maker regarding purchases. The bank might want to know who pays the mortgage. Both may be oblivious to the fact that an elderly grandparent, a disabled toddler, or an unruly teen determines a family's dynamics. It is important that clergy take a broad view of the dynamics of different families and groups and assess how family units collaborate with or undermine one another, how they negotiate conflict, how they try to meet multiple needs, and what compromises are regularly made.

Clergy face a number of challenges when navigating group dynamics. First, not all members of the group will express their opinions. Second, those that do may voice opinions that do not represent the opinions or needs of other members of the group. Third, conflict is inevitable, and group members look to the rabbi to take care of the group. The effectiveness and vitality of all groups depends on their collective flexibility and tolerance. Whether it is a short-term group focused on a specific task, such as a nursery school parents' holiday-planning committee, or a long-term, more general group, such as the synagogue ritual committee, clergy's awareness of these dynamic sub-texts facilitates effective functioning and leadership.

Four group scenarios follow. The first involves a family, the second a small leadership group dealing with a congregational problem, and the third and fourth portray larger community matters.

Example 54. Joyous events become complicated

Eleanor and Herschel Leopold have two adult children, Sally, age 30, and Rebecca, age 27. It is now early February. Sally, a success-ful architect, who married right after college and divorced a year later, has been dating Ephraim for the past three months. Rebecca got married two years ago and is pregnant with the Leopold's first grandchild, due in early July. A week ago, Sally told her parents that she and Ephraim have decided to get engaged. They would like to plan their wedding for June, as they both want an outdoor ceremony, and Ephraim's parents have a seasonal summer busi-ness that gets very busy after July 4th.

Eleanor and Herschel are startled and worried. First, they feel that given Sally's past divorce, three months is not long enough for her to date before deciding on marriage. Second, they wonder how much of Sally's quick decision to get mar-ried is motivated by competitive feelings towards her younger sister who is expecting a baby. A wedding close to Rebecca's due date runs the risk of distracting from both events. Rebecca will not like the idea of walking down the aisle hugely preg-nant or missing the wedding if she gives birth early. Also, the *bris* (circumcision) or other naming ceremony might coincide with the wedding festivities. Lastly, Herschel and Eleanor have allocated a specific sum of money for each of their children's educations and weddings. They have limited funds for a second wedding for Sally and worry about the financial implications of a wedding during the most expensive season.

When the Leopolds suggest that Sally consider a September wedding she becomes hurt and angry. Herschel and Eleanor meet with their rabbi, Daniel Marcus, for advice.

A question to consider

1. How do you assign priorities to the competing agendas within a family?

Discussion

The rabbi listens as Herschel and Eleanor tell the story. His recognition of family dynamics helps him map out the situation. Sally wants her family's full-hearted enthusiasm and support in celebrating her engagement and making plans for a second marriage. Her parents, however, are worried that in her rush to remarry, Sally might make another mistake. Herschel and Eleanor also worry about shortchanging Rebecca, who feels that the birth of her first child deserves the family's full attention. Rabbi Marcus surmises that Eleanor and Herschel are trying too hard to micromanage the diverse agendas of their adult children. He feels that Sally needs to make her own decisions and that his best contribution is to help her parents facilitate how those decisions are made. By modeling calm and balance, the rabbi helps the Leopolds step back to give Sally room to make the best choice she can. The rabbi realizes that a long history of sibling rivalry has set the stage for the current drama. This is not the time to plunge into an exploration of such matters. Rabbi Marcus might speculate to himself or even out loud, depending on his relationship with Herschel and Eleanor, that Sally's timing is not accidental. Sally may want to trump the event of the first grandchild or at least be married before the baby is born. No matter how accurate the rabbi's hunch, resolution of longstanding issues is not feasible at this moment and should not be the current agenda. In fact, Rabbi Marcus deliberately chooses not to dwell on such matters because he understands that doing so would not bring about a better or easier outcome.

Instead, Rabbi Marcus's perspective is pragmatic and focused on the big picture. He advises the Leopold family to step back from straining to make everyone happy and work everything out. He focuses on their report that Sally is eager to make a commitment and that Ephraim seems to be a fine person who treats their daughter well. Regarding the problem of money, the rabbi expresses his opinion that there is no need for Herschel and Eleanor to fully finance a big second wedding. He suggests that they decide on a monetary gift to Sally that fits their budget and then have a conversation with their daughter in which they explain that it is her and Ephraim's choice whether to spend it on a big wedding or something else. Herschel and Eleanor should make clear that whatever the young couple decides, they as parents are excited for them and want to be involved in the celebration.

Rabbi Marcus also addresses the issue of timing. By choosing a June wedding date, Sally is creating a possibility which may not allow for her parents' and sister's full participation. Again, the rabbi suggests that Herschel and Eleanor step back. Sally has the right to choose her wedding date, and she, not her parents, must take responsibility for the potential overlapping events. Sally needs to be prepared that her parents might choose that neither of them are present at her wedding to Ephraim. Herschel and Eleanor might say something like, "We don't have favorites among our two children, but a baby is coming, and that can't be scheduled as precisely as a wedding. We want to participate in both events and celebrate this abundance of joyous occasions. Please factor the unpredictability of childbirth into your decision." Herschel and Eleanor may be clear about their preference, "Our first choice for your wedding is September, as then we can be confident that we will be able to participate fully in both of these wonderful family celebrations."

Rabbi Marcus understands that the Leopolds' long-term concern is for the future relationships between their children. By not weighing in on who is right and who is wrong, Rabbi Marcus gives the family the opportunity to reach an accommodation. This does not mean that he advises that Herschel and Eleanor abdicate responsibility. Rather, the rabbi helps them understand that the current crisis represents a continuation of something that started a long time ago. Right now, the best they can do is step back, get out of the way, and encourage their adult children to behave in accordance with the values with which they were raised. Straining to try and fix matters will not yield a magical solution but more likely result in additional difficulties.

Depending on the outcome of this meeting, Rabbi Marcus, Herschel, and Eleanor might decide to meet again and include the rest of the family. The rabbi might suggest family therapy if the level of tension or anger threatens to destroy basic alliances within the family. The rabbi's role is to remain available and supportive to the entire Leopold family. Rabbi Marcus has conducted himself in such a way that any member of the Leopold family will feel comfortable approaching him in the future.

Example 55. A felon returns to the community

One of Rabbi Kane's congregants, Martin Hecht, a regular attendee of morning *minyan* (prayer group) and a devoted volunteer for youth activities, was charged with and found guilty of downloading images of young teens being sexually exploited. He served several months in prison and, in two weeks, is scheduled to return home on parole. Rabbi Kane knows that the conditions of Martin's release mandate that he see a therapist. In her pastoral visits to the prison, Rabbi Kane discusses the specifics of Martin's re-entry into the synagogue community. Martin understands that he can no longer be involved in youth group work and that he is not allowed to be alone with children in any synagogue-related settings. At the same time, Rabbi Kane must consider whether any of the teens in the synagogue that Martin has had contact with, have been inappropriately solicited or victimized by him.

Rabbi Kane anticipates that Martin's return will provoke many feelings for congregants. In an effort to get a sense of the community's reactions and in order to facilitate Martin's re-entry into the synagogue, she calls for a meeting with the executive committee. Her task is twofold. As rabbi to the entire congregation, she understands that, because of the nature of the crime, many members will be uncomfortable or even fearful of Martin's return. There is reason to worry that synagogue youth who have not stepped forward have been compromised. Rabbi Kane feels a strong sense of responsibility to protect the community's children. At the same time, Martin has served his sentence and, through her pastoral conversations with him, Rabbi Kane believes that Martin has made serious efforts towards religious repentance and needs to re-establish his Jewish life. In this regard, the rabbi wants to forestall the possibility of the community shunning Martin and his family. The executive committee includes Howard, the president, Marion, the vice-president, and Drew, the secretary and treasurer. Rabbi Kane's main goal is to recruit their support by establishing safe policies and a unified approach in what is likely to be a contentious situation.

Rabbi: Thank you all for coming. We are here to talk about a sensitive matter. Some of you might know that Martin Hecht will be returning to the community in two weeks. I have spoken to him and his family extensively, and Martin has agreed that he will not be involved with youth groups or have any interaction with kids. He also understands that in order to reassure the rest of the synagogue, we will have to find a way to enforce this. Our purpose tonight is to discuss how this will work.

Howard: So, I don't like complaining, but the idea of *that* man being back is very upsetting. I'm really angry about this.

Drew: Come on Howard, you can at least say his name.

Howard: I don't want to say his name. You know whom I mean. He was in prison – for what he did to little kids. He doesn't deserve the right to be with us. This guy is pure evil.

Rabbi: I understand that you are upset, Howard. There is no evidence that Martin did anything other than download pictures but I agree that we must act with utmost vigilance and develop a plan for protecting our youth.

Howard: Rabbi, please, don't give us this sympathetic stuff. I am horrified that you would even think of letting Martin back in our community. The idea of him walking around with access to kids playing in the hall or hanging around outside is upsetting. I can't imagine being in morning *minyan* with him, let alone anything else. I really am not sure I can continue my membership if Martin is here.

Rabbi: Howard, this situation has been a challenge for all of us. I believe that we can implement necessary safety measures. We can start with our local police department or Child Advocacy Center. We should also get advice from Martine's parole officer and mental health treatment provider. I think we would also benefit from consulting with an expert to make sure we have the right policies for our synagogue in general. I know of a few organizations that can help. Sacred Spaces focuses on Jewish institutions and GRACE on Christian ones. We might also get ideas from Gundersen National Child Protection Training Center. But I'm hearing that you have a different reaction, and I want to address your feelings.

Howard: Luckily, I'm over the age of 14. Rabbi, don't make it about any one of us. I'm talking about a serious danger to our community.

Drew: The rabbi asked if the rest of us feel threatened. I'm worried about whether we can realistically supervise Martin on our premises. But even more, I'm worried about whether families will feel safe with a convicted pedophile in our midst.

Marion: I share your struggle. My children are part of the community too. I also have ambivalent feelings about someone who has done something so offensive.

Howard: What's the ambivalence? There's only one option. Throw him out!

Drew: Come on, Howard, you are really being extreme.

Howard: No. Rabbi, I want to hear how you would feel coming out into the yard and seeing your kids talking to Martin.

Rabbi: I could tell you that, and I will if you want, but I think it's a better use of our time right now to explore our obligation to a fellow Jew who has committed a serious offense and has been punished and now wants to come back home.

Marion: The rabbi has a point.

Howard: Not here. This is not some random white-collar crime. This is getting off on dirty pictures of kids. Who knows what else he did or might do in the future? What kind of message are we sending?

Rabbi: We are sending a message that a person who has done wrong is still a Jew and a member of our community. And that repentance and return is possible. But of course it is also important to address your very real concern for the safety of our community. But let's be clear about one thing. Our behavior towards Martin will not be punitive. He has served his time and, if further judgment is needed, it will be done by God. Our job is to put in the safeguards we need so that Martin can be here and not pose any threats. I take Martin's past history seriously.

Howard: Yes. This is a real moral dilemma for our community. I respect the value of extending a redemptive hand, even to people whose offenses disgust us. At the same time, we are responsible for keeping our children safe from potential danger.

Marion: How are people supposed to know what the synagogue is doing about Martin?

Rabbi: I need you to convey to people how seriously this matter has been taken. Since Martin was first accused, I have been working to support his family and make sure that they don't feel marginalized by our community. I think we have an obligation to the Hechts and to Martin to integrate him back into the synagogue and also maintain a high degree of surveillance.

Drew: What does that mean specifically?

Rabbi: We need to talk about this more. We need to make sure that when Martin is in the synagogue, he has no contact with youth programs.

Howard: Who is going to make that happen, Rabbi?

Rabbi: For starters, Martin must agree with the conditions we set. We will need to take turns watching him, and we will need to let the community know our specific plans. I'm also anticipating that people will have mixed reactions to this situation. People who know that you are on the executive committee might reach out to you. Please communicate the basics, that Martin will not have any contact with youth and will be under surveillance while he is on the synagogue's premises. Let me know what kind of issues come up, and let's meet again in two weeks.

Howard: Okay.

Drew: Sounds good.

Marion: Let's give it a try.

Questions to consider

1. How do you balance the religious needs of a penitent congregant with the comfort of the community?

2. Should sexual offenses carry more stigma than other forms of misconduct?
3. Who determines safety in your community or organization?

Discussion

Rabbi Kane navigates this complex situation well. She comes into the meeting with a specific rabbinic agenda: to inform a key group, namely the synagogue's executive committee, of Martin's return. Her goal is to secure their support in the face of anticipated communal anxiety and to create a plan. In addition to her religious leadership, Rabbi Kane acts as a strong group facilitator. In this heated discussion, Howard quickly emerges as the divergent, contrary member. Drew and Marion function in structural, sociable capacities, supporting the rabbi's agenda and working towards smoother group function. The meeting would likely have taken quite a different direction if Rabbi Kane had passively waited, rather than assuming a pro-active stance. Specifically, the rabbi validates Howard's concerns but also advances her agenda that differs significantly from Howard's intentions.

Rabbi Kane demonstrates religious leadership by reminding congregants of the Jewish value of repentance. She facilitates the group by permitting members to express raw, negative feelings. She understands that this situation requires a focused action plan in addition to discussion. The rabbi's directive to schedule a follow-up meeting demonstrates that this kind of situation is not resolved in one meeting. It is likely that Howard, or other members of the group, will try to garner support for their positions by discussing the matter with other members of the community. Rabbi Kane will be prepared for phone calls and emails from synagogue members regarding Martin Hecht.

Example 56. A call to action

Over the past several months, local news has focused on illegal Central American immigrants who live on the outskirts of the city. Women in this group seek employment as domestic workers and men as laborers in local construction. One of the men was recently injured on a job site and, because he was afraid of being deported, did not seek medical attention. As a result, the worker died. Subsequent journalistic investigation revealed multiple problems, such as salaries less than minimum wage, lack of health care, and sordid living conditions.

Dr. Ellen Shapiro, the director of the JCC in the area, feels strongly that the JCC should take a public stand on this issue of social justice. While the JCC hires only legal workers, many members utilize the services of illegal immigrants. Because the workers live in the larger community and are subject to exploitation, Dr. Shapiro believes it is the responsibility of the JCC to speak out on this issue. She writes about the matter in the JCC weekly newsletter and asks people to join a committee to plan a day of study and action on issues of social justice and immigration. Dr. Shapiro is surprised by the negative reactions to her plan.

Questions to consider

1. What is your stance on bringing contemporary political or social issues into the Jewish communal sphere?
2. What issues have polarized your community?
3. When is it healthy or productive to discuss polarizing issues in a community?

Discussion

Clergy often take advocacy positions on contemporary issues, though calls to action tend to mobilize strong emotion that invites pastoral intervention. Communities are bound to have differing opinions on clergy's roles vis-à-vis such activities. Some congregants, for example, will applaud clergy for taking the lead to protest social injustice or organize rallies in support of specific Jewish concerns. Other members will disagree with such stances or want their clergy to devote all of their time to counseling, teaching, and cultural or religious programs.

Before Dr. Shapiro writes a piece or announces a program that is likely to cause a stir, she checks in with other members of the staff and/or key board members. If she wants to introduce something that involves a call to action, she prepares for the possibility that her position will be challenged and her actions criticized. She identifies people within the JCC who support her involvement with the cause. A public piece of writing or a sermon on a hot topic should not be the first time that key congregants learn about a controversial initiative. Rather, Dr. Shapiro's essay and call to action should serve to engage the larger membership.

She understands that some people will disagree with her fundamental stance. Others may feel neutral but not want the JCC to be seen as taking a public position. Therefore, before Dr. Shapiro issues a more general call to action, she enlists key members as supporters and formulates an organized plan for community participation. A community action plan must consider the diverse desires of members and be ready to meet opposition. The decision to take on a polarizing position comes at a cost. It is no news to practicing clergy that enormous fallout can ensue from taking unpopular or controversial positions.

Example 57. A discussion arouses strong feelings

The Israel committee at the university Hillel invites a panel of writers and activists who represent diverse opinions regarding the Israeli–Palestinian conflict. Audience members start to clap and boo during the presentations. Before moderating the question and answer portion of the program, Rabbi Jack Stein restates the need for civil discourse. However, after the second question, an argument breaks out.

Questions to consider

1. What is the rabbi's role in this situation?
2. What pastoral consequences should be anticipated when clergy engage in politics?

Discussion

As in the above example, the rabbi must be careful to understand how congregants are likely to respond to political matters that can be contentious. His or her actions are likely to be viewed as favoring one political position and criticizing another. Many rabbis believe that it is not only right to promote a political agenda but that they have an obligation to steer their congregations in the path that they believe is correct. Clergy who take this position must be prepared for the inevitable criticism and potential unruliness that follows. In general, with group encounters on hot topics, clergy should anticipate a wide range of responses. Some members might become tearful or angry, while others may seem neutral or even apathetic. Clergy need to model civil discourse and the respectful consideration of all opinions.

Groups are made up of individuals. Clergy, as leaders of a group, benefit from understanding group dynamics within the community. Additionally, the rabbi needs to consider where congregants might stand on the spectrum of contentious issues. Some are likely to be allies, while others will be neutral or opposed. Most demanding will be those congregants who are so opposed to a stance that they threaten to leave the congregation altogether and try to influence others to leave with them.

Reference

MacKenzie, K. Roy (1990). "Social Roles," in *Introduction to Time-Limited Group Psychotherapy* (Washington, DC: APA Press), pp. 61–74.

Chapter 9

Integrating components to approach complex situations

Up to this point, we have broken down pastoral counseling practices into specific lessons and illustrated these points with focused vignettes. In this chapter, the components from previous chapters are integrated in order to illustrate how to handle more complex situations. In addition, suggestions are provided for helping clergy navigate their own feelings of disappointment or failure when their counseling results in unanticipated outcomes.

Example 58. Pre-marital tension

David Wolfson, 48, calls his rabbi, Shira Kane, and asks her to perform his upcoming wedding to Lisa Margolis, 39. David comes from a religious background but has lapsed in practice and now attends services only sporadically. David has been divorced for many years, and his three children live primarily with their mother in another city. Lisa has not been married before. After congratulating David, Rabbi Kane explains that her policy for officiating at a wedding requires that she and the couple meet for several pre-marital counseling sessions. David agrees and makes a time to come in with his fiancée. Rabbi Kane spends the first 45-minute session getting to know a bit about each of their backgrounds, how they met, what drew them to each other, and how they envision their wedding.

At the next session, the rabbi inquires about David's children and about their plans for having children of their own. David states that he is happy with his three kids and does not feel the need to begin a new family with Lisa. Lisa is taken aback. She had assumed that she and David would have children together.

Questions to consider

1. What is the rabbi's role once a potential source of conflict emerges in a pre-marital counseling session?
2. What should the rabbi do if he/she is the only one who seems to recognize a potential problem?
3. What steps would you take towards resolution of this issue?
4. Would you go ahead and perform the wedding for this couple?
5. Under what conditions would you suggest postponing a wedding?

Discussion

Pre-marital counseling is one of the most important responsibilities of a rabbi who officiates at weddings. Marriage is an important life-cycle event that has profound religious significance even to people who are not consistently observant. The decision to be married by a rabbi demonstrates that the couple wants to incorporate Jewish values into their life together. From the rabbi's side, pre-marital counseling goes beyond planning the wedding. Marriage is a sacred covenant between two people, and the rabbi's participation implies a responsibility to assess the intentions and potential problems of the future partners' commitments.

Rabbi Kane has refined her pre-marital counseling protocol over the years. She is attuned to signs of potential conflict. She is also aware that pre-marital counseling sessions need to be adjusted according to the couple. These include couples in which both members are entering marriage for the first time, couples of different levels of religious observance, couples in which a person is widowed or divorced, and couples with a large age gap. In each interview, Rabbi Kane tries to get to know the prospective spouses better, get a sense of the couple's relationship, and identify the hot-button topics that the couple may or may not have already worked through. She finds that issues that may become problematic later in the marriage present themselves in these conversations. By asking David and Lisa about their desires to start a family, Rabbi Kane uncovers a serious conflict that has implications for their marriage. This is not uncommon. Many people choose to marry and get caught up in the excitement of planning their wedding without working through important issues relating to their marriage. This is why pre-marital counseling sessions are so valuable.

Identifying a basic issue that will likely be a source of conflict in a marriage is sure to generate anxiety. The natural tendency when stumbling into such a thicket is to normalize the omission and not disrupt the happy trajectory of the upcoming wedding. That is not the correct course of action. Clergy's role obligates them to inquire into what it means that a basic issue has not been discussed, let alone resolved, so close to the wedding.

Rabbi Kane meets this pastoral challenge with tact. She hypothesizes that Lisa, who has not been married, is ready to walk down the aisle and has avoided a number of areas that might jeopardize the wedding. David, who has his own sense of urgency to resume the kind of rich family life that he enjoyed prior to the deterioration of his first marriage, has a different vision. Rabbi Kane guesses that David wants to pick up where he left off, with grown children, looking towards the next phase of life when the children are on their own. Like Lisa, he too avoided the issue of having babies in this marriage. During his courtship with Lisa, he did not bring up the matter. While it does not particularly shock David that Lisa wants a child, this is not something he wants to do.

Rabbi Kane understands that she and the couple will not resolve this key issue in a few counseling sessions. More importantly, she does not think that this couple is ready to marry, at least not yet. Stating this directly is unlikely to be helpful and may alienate the couple from her. This might even have an unintended, negative consequence of allowing them to further avoid discussion of the issue. The rabbi will be more effective by asking a series of questions that allow David and Lisa to realize that they must discuss this and other issues prior to marriage. For example, Rabbi Kane might make a general observation that facilitates further exploration of the topic without sounding accusatory: "Lisa, I see that you are upset. I've been assuming that this is not the first time that you and David have had an open discussion about your hopes to have children together … Is this a correct assumption?"

The rabbi deliberately stops here even though she will be tempted to go on. After the rabbi stops talking, there will likely be an uncomfortable silence as her comment was directed to both Lisa and David. It is possible that no one will speak right away. During this pause, Rabbi Kane observes the couple to see if they look at each other, look away from each other, or look to her to dispel the awkward silence. Looking at each other suggests better communication between them. Looking away or towards her for guidance implies discomfort and avoidance. The rabbi waits patiently. She understands that the process of who speaks first yields important information. Eventually David or Lisa might answer, "Of course we have talked about this," to which Rabbi Kane responds, "And what conclusions did you come to?" The rabbi is prepared for the opposite response as well, "Actually, we haven't really spent much time getting into this yet …" In this case, Rabbi Kane uses the opportunity to reinforce her message, "Okay, even though this may have come up as a surprise in our meeting today, I'm glad it did because it's very important for couples planning on marriage to discuss these issues."

Note that each of the rabbi's questions forces the couple to engage with issues rather than avoid them. Clergy's role in pre-marital counseling is to make sure that the couple has discussed the big issues that are must be addressed for a marriage to succeed. Rabbi Kane brings significant wisdom and experience to pre-marital counseling. First, she knows that couples often avoid uncomfortable topics that will lead to confrontation and possibly threaten an engagement. Second, she knows that people often avoid these conversations out of the naïve view that marriage will force an amicable resolution because they will be in it together. If one member of a couple does not want children, and the other one does, this will strain the marriage in the near future.

Having uncovered a serious conflict, Rabbi Kane explains that she would like to meet at least one more time to help Lisa and David explore the matter further. She might say that because she takes the role of performing marriages seriously, she needs to feel more comfortable before officiating at their wedding. In the interim, she urges the couple to parse this further on their own. She suggests that if they cannot come up with a resolution, the option of postponing the wedding is a reasonable choice under the circumstances. By saying this, she conveys the seriousness with which she regards this matter.

The least helpful thing the rabbi can do is to ignore this potential conflict and engage in the same avoidance as the couple, in the hopes that this issue will be resolved after the wedding. That being said, Rabbi Kane may struggle with ambivalence about being the one who calls the wisdom of a potential marriage into question. Lisa and David are likely to be upset with Rabbi Kane for picking up on a problem that they chose to avoid. Rabbi Kane enjoys performing weddings, and she gets pleasure from seeing previously single and divorced people find partners. She may feel sadness and some guilt at casting a shadow on what David and Lisa had hoped would be a happy ending. However, sometimes clergy do feel sad at the outcome of their pastoral intervention. This does not mean that the intervention was wrong. It is important for clergy to know that good pastoral counseling may not provide immediate gratification for either their congregants or themselves.

Example 59. Infidelity in a compromised marriage

Peter and Jill Block, 52 and 51, have been married for 23 years, have two children in college, and are members of Rabbi Marcus's synagogue. Eight years ago, Jill was diagnosed with multiple sclerosis that progressed steadily and then stabilized. She is now in a wheelchair and requires assistance with everyday tasks. Rabbi Marcus has been supportive throughout Jill's illness, and the family is appreciative of the meals and visits organized by the synagogue and the community fund-raising efforts on behalf of MS research and treatment.

One day, Peter calls and makes an appointment to speak with Rabbi Marcus. At the interview, Peter tells the rabbi that the marriage was not good even before Jill got sick, but he tried to make it work until the children were older. Now, the children are in college and Jill's medical condition has stabilized. Peter no longer wants to stay in the marriage. He confesses that he recently became involved with a college girlfriend, who looked him up on Facebook after her divorce, and that he is in love. He becomes tearful as he tells Rabbi Marcus that after all he has been through, he deserves some happiness.

Peter's dilemma is that he wants to maintain his reputation as an upright citizen and honorable husband. He does not know what to do. He does not want his children or the community to condemn him as a horrible person for leaving his wife and engaging in an extramarital relationship. Rabbi Marcus is aware of and sympathetic to the impact that a disabling illness can have on a couple's relationship. At the same time, he recognizes a pattern he has seen in other troubled marriages: poor communication, emotional withdrawal, and, eventually, infidelity. Peter and Jill maintained a bad relationship for years. While Peter claims that he stayed for the sake of the children, he, as well as Jill, may also have been reluctant to confront deeper issues, face loneliness, or face communal stigma. Now, Jill's motivation for staying in the marriage also includes her need for financial and moral support, as well as the fact that her chances of finding a new partner are severely compromised by her multiple sclerosis.

Questions to consider

1. How do you feel about infidelity in a situation of compromised physical or emotional health?
2. Is there any difference between emotional versus physical infidelity? If so, what?
3. How would you advise congregants balancing personal fulfillment and religious/social responsibility?
4. Would you feel differently if the gender roles were reversed?

Discussion

For Rabbi Marcus to appropriately approach this situation, he must evaluate the immediate feelings triggered in him by this story. He must ask himself whether he is repulsed by Peter's disclosure or whether he feels aligned with his congregant's right to the pursuit of happiness. Since Jill is also his congregant, Rabbi Marcus must check in with his feelings about her. Rabbi Marcus's awareness of his countertransference will shape the course of his pastoral counseling.

The rabbi must also quickly assess whether Peter is asking for permission to extricate himself from his marriage. While Rabbi Marcus understands Peter's yearnings for newfound love, Peter must realize that the rabbi's counsel will be informed by traditional religious values such as loyalty, honesty, altruism, and delayed gratification in the service of a higher ideal of fidelity and family integrity. Rabbi Marcus also understands that Peter's choice of coming to him for counsel reflects a conflict that is greater than the decision of whether to separate from his wife. The rabbi responds, "Peter, I understand that living with a disabled person is very difficult, and I also understand that you and Jill have not been happy for many years. However, as you think about extricating yourself from the marriage, let's consider your decision. Let's spend a moment sitting with that."

Rabbi Marcus sees his job as helping Peter separate the complicated issues of being in an unsatisfying marriage, wanting a divorce, and thinking that he is in love. The rabbi advises Peter that it is important to end one relationship before beginning another and also equally important to determine whether the new relationship is not an escape route that will set up its own challenges. For example, were Peter to marry his old girlfriend, might she become suspicious of his capacity for future fidelity in a new marriage given his past history of conducting a clandestine relationship with her? Regarding Peter and Jill's marriage, Rabbi Marcus advises an honest, collaborative process that gives them a final opportunity to communicate their issues to one another and attempt to revive their marriage or split amicably. This is particularly important if Peter wants to have a good relationship with his children, who are likely to sympathize with their mother. The rabbi offers to meet with Peter and Jill. It is possible that during joint counseling, Jill will reveal that she knows about Peter's extramarital involvement and is willing to tolerate it as long as her husband maintains some level of discretion. Having this out in the open may give Peter a chance to reconsider his options. Towards the end of the interview, the rabbi reaffirms his commitment to both Peter and Jill. He is not in a position to control Peter's reputation. By allowing the Blocks to work this through with one another in an open way, Jill is more likely to feel respected and feel good about the couple's ultimate resolution.

Rabbi Marcus is aware that his pastoral involvement does not end here. Whether Peter and Jill seek marriage counseling or eventually divorce, he must stay present as rabbi to both of them and their children.

Example 60. Sudden tragedy in the family

Larry Brader, 39, a dentist, his wife Pearl, 37, a fourth grade teacher in the local religious day school, and their two children, Michael and Ruthie, ages ten and four, are members of Rabbi Marcus's synagogue. Three days ago, while Larry and Pearl were driving home from celebrating their anniversary, a drunk driver ran into their car. Pearl was critically injured. Larry, who was at the wheel, suffered minor bruises. Rabbi Marcus came to the emergency room as soon as he heard about the accident and has been absorbed with the tragedy since. Last night, Rabbi Marcus was asked by the transplant team to advise on organ donation in case Pearl did not survive. She died early the next morning. Although Larry and Pearl created a will when their first child was born, they do not have documents designating advance care directives or health care proxy. Despite Rabbi Marcus's rabbinic counsel supporting donation, Larry could not bring himself to allow the transplant team to harvest her organs.

The funeral is in a few hours. Rabbi Marcus comes over to Larry's house to talk through the upcoming events. Larry is distraught. He asks the rabbi if he made a mistake about the organ donation and whether or not he should bring the kids to the funeral. Larry says that he can't imagine getting through *shiva*, let alone how to manage the rest of his life.

Questions to consider

1. How do you establish priorities in a complex, urgent situation?
2. How important is the issue of organ donation relative to the other problems?
3. What protocols are in place for unexpected crisis or catastrophe in your community?

Discussion

This case illustrates the complicated and varied roles of the community rabbi in a rapidly unfolding situation that demands capable executive function alongside pastoral expertise. From the moment he hears the news of the accident, Rabbi Marcus devotes himself to supporting Larry and Pearl, making sure the children are cared for, and serving as a religious consultant and overall coordinator regarding critical care decisions that concern Pearl. After her death, the rabbi's priorities shift to helping the family navigate the immediate, concrete details of proper care of her body, handling the funeral arrangements, burial, and *shiva*.

Here, the rabbi is acting in his executive role as religious administrator to ensure that this life milestone is handled in a quintessentially Jewish manner. This discussion assumes that the rabbi and synagogue have established protocols for the death of a congregant, such as contacting the *chevra kadisha* (burial society) and funeral home, obtaining a cemetery plot if necessary, and then helping to run a *shiva*. The rabbi must have established relationships with key people to whom he can quickly delegate the many required tasks. Multiple decisions need to be made, such as where Pearl will be buried, whether to delay the funeral to allow out-of-town family to attend, how to involve the children, who should speak, and how to organize the *shiva*. The rabbi does not make these decisions alone but rather consults with Larry to understand his wishes and what Larry thinks Pearl would have wanted. Also important are the concerns of close family members, the maturity of the Brader children, and the community's psychological and counseling resources, especially in the school.

After Rabbi Marcus calls the chairperson of the *chevra kadisha*, his next call is to the principal of the school for support and advice regarding the Brader children and also the entire day school community. The principal serves an important adjunct role to the rabbi. Besides advising Rabbi Marcus on the Brader children, she has a set of decisions to make, including how the school will communicate the news of this sudden death of a parent who is also a popular teacher. Rabbi Daniel Marcus's own children had Pearl as their fourth grade teacher, and he too is shocked by the tragedy of her death. As he works to provide care and guidance, he needs to stay in tune with his own emotions. Conversations with other community professionals such as the principal help provide a network of support for the rabbi and other caregivers.

Hopefully, the principal also has standard operating procedures in place for how to deal with traumatic events, such as a sudden death, in school. This might include a large assembly or small-group discussions. The school psychologist and guidance personnel need to pay attention to how Pearl's death ripples through the community and to be on alert for unusual reactions. After consulting the family, the school will advise as to whether Pearl's current or past students will attend the funeral and how they will make *shiva* visits. The school will also coordinate these visits with teacher chaperones.

After making these calls, Rabbi Marcus focuses his efforts on the Brader family. Larry is distracted, grief-stricken, and guilt-ridden. When speaking with him in the hours just prior to the funeral, the rabbi balances Larry's desire to talk about culpability, existential questions, and the long-term future with the necessity to navigate the immediate situation. Part of the rabbi's triage function is to take a definite counseling stand and urge Larry to let go of his rumination about having decided against organ donation. This may require additional countertransference management on Rabbi Marcus's part if his religious and personal stance is pro-donation. Rabbi Marcus might even verbalize that while he understands that Larry has lingering, uneasy feelings about the choice he made, now is not the time to talk about it. "I will not forget that we need to talk about this. Now our priority is taking care of you and the kids. Let's wait until after the *shiva*, and then this can be our first topic."

Rabbi Marcus's attention is now on preparing for the funeral. Part of every rabbi's work is to accompany congregants through the process of Jewish mourning. However erudite or learned family members may be in matters of Jewish law and custom, a rabbi understands that in the aftermath of death, particularly untimely or sudden death, people's shock often renders them unable to access procedural information that they know in theory but must now deploy in the face of real loss. The rabbi patiently explains rituals and customs appropriate to each family member. This includes what to wear if they will be tearing *kriya* (ripping clothing as a sign of mourning), what happens at the gravesite, and basic *shiva* protocol. Rabbi Marcus knows from experience that religious ritual provides a soothing structure and emotional support in times of devastation and disorder.

The Brader situation also requires that the rabbi have a basic grasp of normal developmental psychology so that he can properly counsel Ruthie and Michael in the immediate and long-term aftermath of their mother's death. The decision as to whether children should attend a parent's funeral and burial takes into account children's ages, personality, and maturity level. Generally speaking, being present at these formal ceremonies helps children by giving them an experience that lends reality to an unimaginable event. Very young children, below the age of five, however, cannot comprehend death or sustain mourning. At the same time that they are involved in mourning rituals in age appropriate ways, children need regular reassurance that they are safe and will be cared for. Rabbi Marcus makes sure that a close friend or relative, other than Larry or Pearl's parents and siblings, who may themselves be too preoccupied in their mourning to attend to the needs of the children, is with Michael and Ruthie throughout the funeral and burial. Similarly, during the *shiva*, they will need caretakers, breaks from being in the main *shiva* room, and play dates. The school can help organize these visits and also communicate to parents in the community that the Brader children need the company of their friends and that playfulness is appropriate and necessary for them.

Rabbi Marcus visits multiple times during *shiva* and pays attention to how Larry and the children are doing. He notes what Larry talks about, such as the organ donation issue. If Larry were to continue to talk about this topic extensively, the rabbi might interject a comment that does not encourage exploration, such as, "You made the best decision you could at the time." The pastoral role here is similar to that of a grief counselor. Rabbi Marcus reassures Larry that reactions such as guilt, sleeplessness, nightmares, intrusive thoughts, and emotional numbness are natural, normal reactions to trauma and are not a cause for alarm. The educated rabbi knows that such responses in the immediate aftermath of loss do not require a grief counselor but rather reassurance.

Rabbi Marcus also understands the protective cocoon that *shiva* offers is time-limited. Once the week ends, resuming normal life will be very painful for Larry. The rabbi checks in frequently with Larry and the children via phone calls and brief visits. While Rabbi Marcus is prepared to discuss Larry's decision not to donate Pearl's organs, he does not initiate such discussion. Rather, the rabbi provides a safe, non-judgmental space for Larry and the children to contemplate any religious questions, such as "Why do terrible things happen to good people?" and "Where is my mommy now?"

It is important for the rabbi to know that in the normal course of bereavement, time does heal and that the intensity of loss, helplessness, confusion, and grief abates. Guilt may be a barrier that stands in the way of the resolution of symptoms after trauma and loss. In this case, for example, if Larry continues to berate himself for not avoiding the accident, the rabbi might say, "Although you drove the car, it was a drunk driver who was responsible for this accident, and you were not the drunk driver."

While, on the surface, being a driver of the vehicle provides a rationale for guilt, this response should be limited. If Larry continues to blame himself for not having averted the accident or ruminates about the organ donation issue months later despite attempts at consolation, Rabbi Marcus guesses that more complex issues may be at play. He understands that Larry's extended bereavement will seriously impact Ruthie and Michael. The rabbi listens for information that supports this hypothesis. When bereavement occurs in a normal manner, existential questions lose their acuity over time and recede. If Larry continues to raise questions of existential guilt and confesses, for example, that while driving on the night of the accident he had been preoccupied with some issue from work, or that he was looking at a text, or that he and Pearl had been fighting in the car and he didn't see the oncoming vehicle in his lane, it would indicate that Larry would benefit from psychotherapy. The rabbi does not attempt to provide psychotherapy himself but rather puts his effort into facilitating an appropriate referral. Similarly, if Pearl's death re-activates unresolved issues from Larry's earlier life, he should be referred to a mental health professional to work through them. The rabbi's job is to navigate the here and now while making room for new details to emerge that might explain a complicated bereavement and then help the congregant work through this in an appropriate setting.

Example 61. Illness and decision-making

Bruce Markowitz, a 78-year-old member of Rabbi Shira Kane's synagogue, has metastatic colon cancer. He lives at home with his wife, Anita. Their two adult children, Marcy and Carl, who do not get along, visit regularly. Over recent years, Bruce Markowitz told Anita and their children, "I don't want to live hooked up to machines." He has been very private about his illness and did not involve anyone outside the family. Carl tried to initiate conversations with his father, mother, and sister about getting Bruce to write out his wishes for a health care proxy and advance medical directives, but they resisted acknowledging the seriousness of the situation and insisted that it was not yet necessary.

One night, while sleeping at home with Anita, Bruce Markowitz has trouble breathing. In a panic, Anita calls 911. Her husband is brought by ambulance to the hospital, where he is intubated for respiratory distress. During the next few hours, Mr. Markowitz's condition deteriorates; his blood pressure begins to drop, he slips in and out of consciousness, and his kidneys show signs of failure.

Marcy and Carl rush to the hospital. By mid-morning Carl calls Rabbi Kane and informs her that Bruce is in the ICU. Rabbi Kane arrives half an hour later and finds the siblings arguing outside their father's room. Anita is sitting in an armchair next to her husband, crying quietly. Rabbi Kane asks the family to fill her in. Marcy reports that her own rabbi's opinion is that her father, as a devoted Jew, should get maximal medical interventions, including staying in the ICU on a ventilator and starting dialysis. Carl adamantly opposes this position, as he feels it violates their father's wishes. In the meantime, the hospital is pressed for ICU beds. As a community rabbi and part-time chaplain, Rabbi Kane is well known to the hospital staff. The ICU director asks her to intervene and clarify what the Markowitz family wants for Bruce.

Questions to consider

1. What is your own position regarding end-of-life decision-making?
2. Are you personally prepared with advance life directives for yourself? Have you appointed a health care proxy for a circumstance in which you can no longer speak for yourself? Have you spoken about this issue in your community?
3. Would your reactions to the case be different if Bruce did not have an underlying terminal illness?
4. How would you deal with the family conflict in this situation?

Discussion

The Markowitz crisis sits at the nexus of Jewish law, medical ethics, and pastoral care. Rabbi Kane is thrust into a leadership position in a rapidly changing picture with multiple potential congregants, including Bruce Markowitz, his wife, his adult children, and the hospital staff. Her initial goal is to organize a hierarchy of priorities. Rabbi Kane decides that she must first sit down with the family, establish a basic alliance with each member, and assess each person's understanding of the situation. Rabbi Kane goes over to the bed, takes Mr. Markowitz's hand, and introduces herself, "Bruce, it's Rabbi Shira Kane. I'm here to visit you." Mr. Markowitz appears unresponsive to words and touch. Rabbi Kane continues to speak to her congregant in the presence of his wife and children, saying, "Bruce, I'm sorry that you are having such a hard time. I want you to know that Anita, Marcy, Carl, and I are here together to see you through this. We are going to go outside your room now to talk in the lounge."

Rabbi Kane now applies her efforts to shoring up the fractured family and appraising the situation. She asks each of the Markowitz family members to spell out their understanding of Bruce's condition and his wishes regarding advance life directives. When Marcy and Carl begin to squabble over "the right thing to do," Rabbi Kane suggests that they call in Bruce's doctor to get an updated assessment of their father's condition and prognosis. While they wait for the doctor, Rabbi Kane excuses herself briefly in order to cancel her appointments for the rest of the afternoon because she can tell that this time-sensitive situation will demand her full attention for several hours.

Next, Rabbi Kane invites Mr. Markowitz's ICU nurse to join the Markowitz family in the patient lounge. Rabbi Kane explains that Judaism values the sanctity of life and has specific laws regarding end-of-life care. The rabbi elaborates that religious and medical judgment is required as to whether to implement invasive medical procedures that might prolong life but have risks. Rabbi Kane acknowledges that Marcy and Carl came into the discussion with different opinions. "I understand that you each have your own points of view, your own religious counsel, and certainly your own history and relationship with your dad. What's important right now is that we work together with your mom to make the best decision from the perspectives of Jewish tradition and medical science in order to honor your father's welfare and your future as a family. These are values I know that he cares about."

Bruce Markowitz's doctor arrives and confirms that Bruce's condition is indeed declining. His assessment is that Bruce will not recover from this crisis and that instituting dialysis will extend his life for a short while longer in an increasingly debilitated state. The doctor encourages Anita, Marcy, and Carl to "let go of the medical heroics and stay with your husband and dad as he leaves us."

Anita turns to Rabbi Kane and says, "I don't know what to do. Carl and Marcy have to decide." Rabbi Kane suggests that the family sit quietly together for a few moments as they integrate the information and feelings of the preceding hours. She asks if she might read some passages from Psalms out loud that speak to the intense experience of people in dire straits. Carl murmurs, "If only Mom hadn't called 911. If only they hadn't put him on the ventilator to start with. We should just take dad off the respirator." Rabbi Kane gently but firmly interjects, "Carl, it's so hard when someone is alone with a person they love and that person is suffering. Your mother did the best she could. And once a person is on a respirator, Jewish law is very protective about discontinuing life-sustaining support."[1]

Marcy nods. She agrees not to implement dialysis or other heroic measures. Bruce regains consciousness for a few moments later in the afternoon but slips into a coma and dies two days later. Anita, Marcy, and Carl are present and supportive throughout the funeral and *shiva*. They thank Rabbi Kane for her presence and active leadership through this harrowing time.

The Markowitz family situation confirms for Rabbi Kane the need for congregants of all ages and family constellations to become more educated about end-of-life decisions. She convenes a committee to create a program called "Honoring Choices," so that members of the community engage in learning and guided discussion about end-of-life issues that are so often neglected because of discomfort. Over the course of three evenings, congregants study Jewish texts on end-of-life issues and familiarize themselves with legal documents regarding health care proxies and advance life directives. The program includes small-group conversations. Numerous congregants come over to thank Rabbi Kane for giving them the opportunity to talk about a subject that is so often avoided. They tell her that even though it was hard, they feel closer to the people in their small groups and more at ease with their own mortality.

Note

1 Halachic authorities debate whether medical interventions should be taken to extend the life of a terminally ill patient who is conscious and experiencing pain. Some authorities require that all life-extending measures be taken (see Rav Eliezer Waldenberg, *Tzitz Eliezer*, vol. 10, 25:6 and Bleich 2002, 167–185). However, most authorities rule that natural death should be allowed to take its course and that medical intervention is not only not required but may actually be forbidden (see Rav Yosef Shalom Elyashiv, quoted in Nishmat Avraham, Yoreh Deah, vol. 4, 339:2; Rav Shlomo Zalman Aurbach, *Minchat Shlomo*, vol. 1, 91:24; Rav Zalman Nechemia Goldberg, *Emek Halakha*, vol. 2, pp. 64–83; Rav Moshe Feinstein, *Iggrot Moshe, Hoshen Mishpat*, vol. 2, 73:1, YD, vol. 2, 174:3; Rav Shlomo Vosner, *Shevet HaLevi*, vol. 6, 179). If the patient is unconscious, the matter is more contentious (see Linzer 2013 for an overview of these issues). The general principle in halacha is that one may not hasten a death, but one should also not stop a natural death from taking place. On the basis of this, many halachic authorities have ruled that it is permitted to withhold most forms of medical intervention from a patient who is terminally ill, but it is forbidden to withdraw treatment because the latter constitutes hastening death. Many treatments can be interrupted even after they had been initiated by simply choosing not to re-administer them. In the case of a ventilator, however, the treatment continues without the need for ongoing maintenance. In addition, because it takes over a bodily function, it might be halachically considered a part of the person's body. Thus, the legal consensus is that a person may not be taken off of a ventilator once such treatment has begun (see Rav Moshe Feinstein, *Iggrot Moshe*, YD 3:132 and Rav Shlomo Zalman Aurbach, as quoted in Steinberg 1993. However, as Rabbi Dov Linzer explains, "in the case of a terminally ill patient, most authorities would allow the cessation or gradual altering of a treatment when such actions would not lead to the immediate death of the patient, even though death may occur within a few hours. This would not be considered hastening death, merely the cessation of a therapy." (See also the 1995 ruling of Rav Yosef Shalom Elyashiv, Rav Shlomo Zalman Aurbach, Rav Shlomo Vosner, and Rav Nisim Karelitz, recorded in Steinberg 2008.)

References

Bleich, J. David (2002). *Judaism and Healing: Halakhic Perspectives* (Jersey City, NJ: Ktav Publishing).

Linzer, Dov (2013). "Treatment of Terminally Ill Patients According to Jewish Law," *Virtual Mentor, American Medical Association Journal of Ethics* 15.12 (December): 1081–1087.

Steinberg, A. (1993). "Establishing the Moment of Death: An Overview of the Positions," *Assia* 53–54: 5–16.

Steinberg, A. (2008). "The Halachic Basis of 'The Dying Patient Law'," *Jewish Medical Ethics and Halacha* 6.2 (October): 30–40, http://98.131.138.124/articles/JME/JMEM12/JMEM.12.3.asp, accessed June 20, 2016.

Epilogue
Going forward

Much of the material covered in this book focuses on difficult situations that clergy will encounter in everyday life. It may be hard to imagine that involvement in human suffering can be rewarding and result in spiritual growth, personal maturity, and wisdom. By implementing the skills and techniques outlined in this book, clergy's competence and confidence will increase such that interventions on behalf of congregants become increasingly fulfilling.

The practice of pastoral counseling thrives when clergy are mindful of their responsibility to continually hone their skills and check in with their own feelings. The rabbi's task is to use the principles and methodology offered here in a way that suits his/her own individual personality and practice. Active, compassionate, non-judgmental listening is an important skill to practice so that clergy can create external and internal climates of pastoral hospitality and self-awareness. So, too, clarification of professional and personal boundaries requires constant attention and vigilance on the part of clergy.

This book was written to help clergy navigate complex pastoral situations with confidence, compassion, and wisdom. This journey arose from our roles as teachers, educators, and clinical supervisors. Going forward, readers should feel more equipped to help alleviate suffering and deepen joy in the context of religious life. Honing the craft of pastoral counseling is a journey requiring ongoing curiosity and wonder at the depths of human suffering and the extraordinary capabilities troubled people have for resilience and growth.

About the authors

Dr. Michelle Friedman is a psychiatrist and psychoanalyst in private practice, the chair of Pastoral Counseling at Yeshivat Chovevei Torah Rabbinical School (YCT), and Associate Clinical Professor of Psychiatry at the Icahn School of Medicine at Mount Sinai Hospital in New York City. Dr. Friedman has been involved in bridging religious life and mental health issues for over 30 years. She has spearheaded educational initiatives on a variety of topics, including religious identity, postpartum depression, and sexuality. In 1998, Dr. Friedman was invited to develop a pastoral counseling curriculum for YCT in order to prepare Modern Orthodox rabbis to meet the challenges of contemporary community leadership. Much of this book comes out of that teaching experience and her ongoing contact with graduates of YCT and other rabbinical seminaries.

Dr. Rachel Yehuda is a Professor of Psychiatry and Neuroscience at the Icahn School of Medicine at Mount Sinai where she directs the Traumatic Stress Studies Division She is also the Director of the Mental Health Care Center at the James J. Peters Veterans Affairs Hospital in the Bronx. She founded and directed many clinical treatment programs including the Specialized Treatment Program for Holocaust Survivors and their Families, the Children's After Trauma Care and Health Program (CATCH) and the 9/11 Psychotherapy Program at Mount Sinai. She has been an active researcher of post-traumatic stress disorder and resilience and is the recipient of numerous grants and awards for her work.

Recognizing that rabbis are often called on to respond to trauma and tragedy, Dr. Friedman recruited Dr. Yehuda to help develop the pastoral program. Over the last decade, they have collaborated on several studies on Jewish life and mental health. These include a survey on sexual life for observant Jewish women, sexual abuse in the Jewish community, and a comparison of religious repentance and psychotherapy. Their friendship and long history of collaboration have made this project a natural extension of their shared commitment to Jewish life and expertise in mental health care and clinical research.

Index

688002